HOW TEXAS POLITICS REALLY WORKS

How Texas Politics Really Works

Kevin Bailey

Bob Locander

Richard C. Shaw

For permission, write to
3 Friends Publishing
403 Sulky Trail
Houston, TX 77060

First Edition

ISBN: 978-1-974-2695-1-8

Cover Design: Alan McCuller, *www.Mc2graphics.com*

Interior Design: Vivian Freeman, *Yellow Rose Typesetting*

Printed in the United States of America

Published by
Lone Star Productions
13820 Methuen Green
Dallas, TX 75240
Contact: 972-671-0002

Dedicated to

Allen Vogt

Historian, democrat, and Friend

TABLE OF CONTENTS

About the Authors

After leaving college teaching, **Kevin Bailey** took a position in Houston city government as the chief of staff for Councilmember Dale Gorczynski. In 1990 Bailey ran and won an election to the Texas House of Representatives for District 140. During his 18 years as a legislator in Austin, he chaired the House Committees on Urban Affairs and General Investigating and Ethics. KB was one of the co-founders of the Legislative Study Group in the House. Holding political science degrees from the University of Texas at El Paso and Sam Houston State University, Bailey is now on the faculty at Houston Community College.

Bob Locander holds a Ph.D. in political science from the University of New Mexico. His professional articles and reviews have appeared in Presidential Studies Quarterly, The American Political Science Review, and The Texas Journal of Political Science. Locander has been a long-time faculty member at Lone Star College—North Harris. He has also taught courses on politics at Lamar University, the University of Houston, and the University of Houston-Downtown. "Tales from the Unionside" is a regular political column BL writes for a quarterly labor newsletter.

For over 43 years, **Richard C. Shaw** was active in the Texas union movement. Shaw retired in 2016 from his position as the Secretary-Treasurer of the Harris County AFL-CIO Council. Prior to his 1995 election to the labor council, he had been the president of the Houston Federation of Teachers. After leaving HFT, RS held posts with AFSCME Local 1550 as a business representative and as an executive director, in addition to serving as a Vice President of the Texas AFL-CIO. Shaw has also worked in government for the City of Houston and is an election judge for Harris County voting Precinct 165.

PREFACE

The idea to write a short introduction to Texas politics for general readers and students came about as a result of a phone call. One future author (KB) called another (BL) to measure his level of interest in joining a group of professors in writing a Texas government college textbook. As we discussed the possibility, both authors began to convince themselves of how bad an idea this was.

As colleagues at North Harris County College in the 1980s, our old complaints began to be resurrected and haunted us again. The major textbook publishers only wanted formula books with glossy pictures, tables, charts, and inserts with sticker shock prices on the cover—better to make students poorer and no more wiser.

The thought came to us that we should break the textbook market mold and head in a different direction. Why not write a realistic introduction to Texas politics with a kick? If toes were stepped on, so be it. Our goal was to write a book that would be short, sweet, and cheap. We never considered contacting the major publishing companies, because their preferences in textbooks ran to long, bland, and expensive.

As the two of us continued our discussions, we decided to seek out a third author (RS) to complete our writing team. When asked to join the project, he paused for a moment reflecting and said, "What you want in a book is some good-old fashioned Texas truth-telling." Exactly! We three authors have known each other for over 35 years.

Each of us comes from a different political vantage point or place: state legislator, college professor, and labor advocate.

With over 100 combined years of engagement in Texas politics, we share many things in common, but we are not political triplets. Much of this book was written during the 2016 presidential election race, and many conversations took place among us about the diabolical Don, Lyin' Ted, little Marco, crooked Hillary, and Uncle Bernie. On November 8, we authors went in three different presidential directions.

From disunited views on national politics, however, came a united view about the structure, purpose, and powers associated with the Texas political system. Taking our lead from James Lamare, author of *Texas Politics: Economics, Power, and Policy,* we openly embraced the elite perspective or model as the best way to explain *How Texas Politics Really Works.*

As a student at the University of Texas at El Paso, Kevin Baily took a political science course from Professor Lamare and was no doubt influenced by him. Lamare's student would go on to serve 18 years in the Texas House of Representatives, where the reality of the professor's theories were confirmed in practice in legislative session after session.

While Lamare's model influenced the book's perspective, it was another author whose work had an impact on the book's format. As a Texas college professor, Bob Locander has seen many changes in students and books over the past 40 years. Just like President Donald Trump, many students today are nonreaders. While it used to be said that readers are leaders, Trump challenges this idea and many students are like the president in that they hate to read anything beyond 140 characters. Even today's English majors seldom get to the "peace" in Tolstoy's great novel. It was partly for this reason and the hope that general readers might be willing to give a short book a try that we watched our page count. In choosing brevity, we followed a template that Charles Peters utilized in his book, *How Washington Really Works.*

In its first edition, the Peters' book, consisting of eight chapters and 135 pages, was very popular among BL's students in an introductory government class. While the organization and title guided us, our work is different from his in subject and tone. We tried to draw on our collective strengths to produce a book that is different from any other Texas politics text in print. *How Texas Politics Really Works* is many books in one. First, we drew on our own personal experiences and political involvements in Lone Star politics as government insiders and outsiders. Second, we tried to stay grounded in political science and history where we could utilize national and state examples to better inform the reader. Third, this point of view book will not be everyone's cup of tea. A teaching colleague of KB used to say that he did not like to be around political scientists as they were always bringing him "bad news." The bad news of political science based on academic research has a way of bursting the bubbles of the naïve and destroying the falsehoods of partisans.

While we think of ourselves as three amigos out to inform citizens of the way things really are in Texas, others might see us as three bad hombres who have been out in the sun too long. To our friends and foes alike, we say that we have tried to give an honest appraisal of Lone Star politics as we have witnessed it from three different angles. As over 65 authors, we like to quote the late Maggie Kuhn, founder of the Gray Panther movement on the value of growing old, "Being 65…becomes a crossroads. We said, we have nothing to lose (at this age), so we can raise hell." It is time for the baby boomers in Texas to display no fear of the state political and economic establishment and to speak truth to power. For the young and the middle-aged, it is our hope that this book will get you thinking about questioning authority and realizing that the public interest is seldom the same as the private interests controlling Austin today.

Kevin Bailey (KB)
Bob Locander (BL)
Richard C. Shaw (RS)
Houston, Texas
July, 2017

Acknowledgments

In order to get this work into print, we had to lean on colleagues, friends, and family for encouragement and support. The many comments we received, both positive and negative, were helpful in the writing and the revising of the book. For those who said that they liked the authors but hated the book, we are glad that you still like us.

We wish to thank the following colleagues and friends for reading various chapters of the book: Gary Brown, Jennifer Crooks, Tony Diaz, John Dobelman, Alan Hall, Ray Hill, Michael McFarland, Danel Olson, and Ron Trowbridge. Special thanks and praise go out to Allen Vogt and Jan Locander for their sound historical and editorial suggestions. A last word of thanks to Vanessa Lopez who was our "Word" master.

CHAPTER ONE

POWER IN TEXAS

Texas politics, like all politics, is the struggle for power. What political scientist Hans Morgenthau once said about world politics is equally true and then some for politics in Texas. The political players in the Lone Star State play "hard ball" and take no prisoners. Politics in Texas is a big boy's game controlled by economic elites outside of state government. These economic notables know that the stakes are high and they play to win at all costs.

It was V.O. Key, Jr., author of *Southern Politics*, who captured the political essence of the Lone Star State when he wrote that, "Texas is concerned about money and how to make it..." While people looking at the Texas state flag see the Lone Star, the rich and powerful have always known that behind the Star is a huge dollar sign. For some readers, our characterization of elites and the state will seem extreme, but let us explore how Texas political scientists have answered the question, "Who has the power in Texas?"

Putting aside for now a specific meaning for the term "power," the various answers to the question concerning power and Texas break down along two explanatory lines or models identified as pluralist theory and elite theory. A few well-intentioned souls have suggested that the people of Texas hold the "power," but this notion is widely rejected within the social science community as a wishful fiction at best and a child's tale at worst.

If the people of Texas do not have power, who does? It is within academia that a great debate about this question has been waged over the years within the fields of sociology and political science. For sociologists, many advance elite theory as the best response to the "who has power" question, while a great number of political scientists have favored pluralist theory. The main point of agreement between the elite and the pluralist theories is that elites, the few, and not the people, the many, are in charge of things. Where the disagreement exists between these two theories is over the number of elites, single or multiple.

Pluralist theorist Robert Dahl would look at Texas and say that many elites or interest groups in the state determine government outcomes. For pluralists like Dahl, today's interest groups are carrying out what Thomas Jefferson and small "d" democrats hoped that the people would take on for themselves. While the people of Texas are neither active nor interested nor informed about civic matters in the way Jefferson hoped they might be, it is the multiple elites or dominant interests which will act, react, and impact the policymaking process within all Texas government branches.

The pluralist portrait of the Austin power arrangement is a constant, either stated openly or quietly implied, in most Texas government textbooks. This standard orientation can be as distorting as the "two sides to every story" approach of establishment or corporate media reporters in covering public affairs. No Texas book has gone as far as Robert Dahl did in offering up the title, *Pluralist Democracy in the United States*, for his introductory book on American politics, but many Texas authors have stepped up close to this line.

It is widely understood that for students and general readers what textbook writers do is to synthesize the work of the subject field under study. Textbooks do matter, however, as these introductions to Texas politics and government may be the first formal impression that a college student or adult reader receives about the Lone Star political system. Since 2013 the state of Texas has mandated that all higher education students, irrespective of major, must complete a semester long course on Texas government as a graduation requirement.

In surveying the content of Texas texts, many are solid and politically safe descriptions of state politics that are more likely to put good students to sleep and average students into a coma. The pages of today's Texas government books will not ignite any political flames to bring about a call for firing those radical University of Texas professors bent on brainwashing impressionable freshmen.

While textbook authors are not part of any elite conspiracy to bring about political conformity and status quo acceptance, these authors know that controversial positions and the questioning of establishment legitimacy are not what major textbook publishers are looking for and printing. It is the sanitized and airbrushed view of Texas politics that makes it onto the shelves of college bookstores.

Lamare's Texas Elite Model

Was the just the facts approach of Texas politics books always this way? The simple answer is "No." As a matter of record, the elite theory of Lone Star politics appeared in multiple editions of James Lamare's introductory textbook, *Texas Politics: Economics, Power, and Policy,* which was in print back in the 1980s and the 1990s. Lamare's work paralleled the national writing of Thomas Dye, author of *The Irony of Democracy,* who presented an uncommon introduction to American government. What Lamare did at the state level and Dye did at the national level was to advance an elite interpretation of politics and government. Despite what some critics have said, elite theory is not conspiracy theory, where shadowy figures behind closed doors attempt to keep the truth from we the people and to pull the strings attached to government officials on the public stage.

James Lamare's Texas vision of economic elites unfolds in three separate sections within the "Introduction" of his book. He first sets out to identify who the elites are. Lamare's elites are the business leaders overseeing the operations of the major corporate interests in the Lone Star State. His second point about these elites is that they are in complete agreement about the economic big picture in Texas where company profits trump all. The third thing Lamare indicates about elites is the close ties that they maintain through their business dealings, private club memberships, and church connections.

How Elites Control Texas Government

After identifying elites and their world, Lamare next goes on to point out the four ways in which the top one percent insures that Texas government will do no harm to the interests of the upper class. Elite control over Austin begins by recruiting and backing elite-friendly political candidates to run for state office. Second, elites do all they can to influence the governor and the state Senate into appointing and confirming government personnel with an "Elites First" outlook. After getting elite sponsored elected and appointed officials into power, economic notables put on a comprehensive lobbying effort directed toward state decision makers to make the right call. Finally, Lamare sees the highly decentralized Texas government structure as ideal for elites' intent on managing the opaque settings of legislative committees, bureaucratic meetings, and judicial hearings.

Following the identification of elites and their world and how they control government mechanisms, Lamare completes the depiction of his Texas elite model by addressing policy outcomes or decisions. The first point he underscores is that state government actions regularly benefit the few but not always at the expense of the many. There are some instances when the public wins a favor or two, but these "wins" have been few and far between over a number of years. Next, Lamare does not believe that the people of Texas matter much in having a say over state actions. The third and final result of Lone Star elite-government relations concerns political change and how it comes about. For change to happen, it must be in the direct interests of elites with little cost to them. Changing things to benefit working people does occur, but is a side effect following the serving of the upper class. Unlike the pluralists' view of policy outcomes being a balanced exchange among interested participants, elite theory posits very little for the masses or ordinary citizens as they end up with one or two slices of the policy bread or go hungry in the process.

The idea of economic elites in charge of government goes back to the American Founding Fathers in the U.S. experience and to Plato and Aristotle in Ancient Greece who believed in philosopher-kings and enlightened aristocrats directing things with the masses having little say. For the 55 delegates at Philadelphia in 1787, it only made sense that men of wealth and breeding should be in charge. With the best and the brightest heading the government, the role of the masses would be relegated to spectator status or political bystanders who would be called on to pay taxes and fight the enemies of the state.

The underlying thesis of *How Texas Politics Really Works* is that James Lamare's economic elite rule model is more right than wrong in describing power in Texas. It is only within the past few years that the Occupy Movement on the left side and the Tea Party on the right side of the Texas political spectrum have made any headway in influencing public opinion that the great majority of people have little effect on what transpires in Austin or Washington. What is an interesting development today is how many people are realizing that American democracy looks more like a

United States plutocracy, and this situation generally has been the historic Texas political condition whether or not the Democrats or Republicans held governmental power in Austin.

What is Lamare's view of Texas state government? Like other elite theorists, such as C. Wright Mills and G. William Domhoff, Lamare believes that the few and not the many make the major decisions affecting the lives of over 28 million Texans. For Lamare, Texas government is of, by, and for wealthy elites. This view of state government is exactly what Joseph Stiglitz, author of *Rewriting the Rules of the American Economy,* has been saying about the national government in his critique of Washington as a place where the political and economic game has been fixed by those with great riches. What American middle class people are waking up to is life within a rigged economy where wealthy and powerful individuals do not miss many political coin flips as it is "heads" elites win and "tails" the people lose.

While many average have-some and have-not Texans avoid political participation, the life-altering Austin game of politics goes on for the have-mores and the haves of the state. It is common to think of societies consisting of the haves or the elites and have-nots or the masses. We will employ this dichotomy from time to time in the book, but we will also incorporate a quadripartite view of Texas and America made up of the have-mores, haves, have-somes, and have-nots. The easiest way of identifying our four-way division is through the use of 2016 federal income figures with the have-mores or top one percent earners making $699,999 and above. The haves are the next 19 percent who made at least $143,000 plus. The have-somes had incomes ranging from $48,400 to the bottom of the have range. The have-nots are people in the bottom 40 percent of the income scale going down from $48,399 to zero dollars.

The political fix in Texas and America comes in through direct and indirect control of the have-mores and haves over the legislative, executive, and judicial branches of government. Elites try to dominate all aspects of the political process from selecting candidates, financing campaigns, lobbying office-holders, influencing government appointments, and shaping public policy outcomes. On only rare occasions will the "David" majority defeat the "Goliath" minority on matters of economic and political importance. These "David" wins do occur, but the results often are symbolic victories more than substantive wins for the have-somes and have-nots.

Power: Its Two Faces

This chapter began with the Morgenthau-applied statement that Texas politics is the struggle for power. The concept of power has been a central point of intellectual inquiry for political scientists over time. Trying to understand this concept is what distinguishes political science from the other social sciences. So what is power? For years it was believed that power equated with influences and outcomes. Richard Neustadt, author of *Presidential Power,* has written that presidential power was the power of a chief executive to persuade other Washington officials to do what he wanted them to do without having to issue direct commands or orders.

The idea of an executive or leader using personal skills to accomplish goals has been stated best by Robert Dahl in his identification of two actors "A" and "B" in a political setting. Dahl indicates that "A," an individual or group, has power over "B," another individual or group, to the extent that "A" can get "B" to do something that "B" would not have done without "A's" intervention. This "achievement" sense of power is how most people commonly think of power as the movers and shakers go about getting their way in any setting. Using a variety of means, Texas elites achieve their political, economic, and social goals over the masses or ordinary people. While this is the "visible" face of Peter Bachrach and Morton Baratz's "Two Faces of Power," it is not the only way that elites control things in Texas.

For years the Texas establishment or economic elites owned

state government through a state Democratic Party that elected all of its gubernatorial candidates from Richard Coke in 1874 to Dolph Briscoe in 1974. During this 100 year period, both houses of the Legislature and the state courts were safely in Democratic hired hands doing the policy chores of their upper class masters. This first face of power in which an individual or an interest group prevails over others is what Bachrach and Baratz identify as "visible." This visible face appears when the champion wears the crown for all to see, admire, or envy. Getting one's way, achieving one's goals, and coming in first are all illustrations of this type of power exercise.

But what of the "invisible" face of power? This face is right in front of us, although many people have trouble seeing the ghost face of power exercised by the few at the top of the social structure. The goal of every Super Bowl champion is to win the following season and the season after that. In a similar way, elites' controlling of the political and economic status quo year after year is their greatest exercise of power today.

Preventing or rechanneling change to an acceptable level is what Texas elites do in an invisible way. Demands for change coming from the Green Party on the left, the moderate middle in the center, or the Tea Party on the right are processed through a status quo filtering machine. Some left, center, and right proposals will be rejected outright as unacceptable to the few, while other ideas will be gutted with just an outer shell remaining of the original proposal. The best way for elites to defeat something not in their interests is for the top dogs to accept a watered-down version of an underdog proposition and to allow mass leaders to claim a symbolic victory of sorts. It is easy to see how the 1957 Civil Rights Act was not much of a win for equal rights, but how the Civil Rights Act of 1964 was a substantial victory for Martin Luther King Jr. and thousands of activists concerned about equal opportunity and justice in America.

Like C. Wright Mills's *Power Elite* at the national level, the Lone Star establishment is not involved in ironing out every new wrinkle in the state social and economic fabric. Why worry about small things when a symbolic change or slight deviation from the norm will not cause any alteration of who has power and control. For Mills's national notables, the big picture concerns after World War II dealt with the dominance of the capitalistic economic system at home, and the United States control over an imperial, anti-Communist foreign policy network throughout the world.

For the Texas establishment, the top concerns from the time of the 1876 Texas Constitution until today have been: to limit the powers of state government, to keep taxes low and regressive, to minimize the economic regulation of business, to insure that government does as little as possible to help ordinary Texans, and to make it as difficult as possible for low income folks and people of color to participate in the political system.

How have economic elites been able to get away with doing so little for the masses? It is the genius of elites that they embrace stances of flexibility and pragmatism when serious challenges to their authority crop up. Had elites been at the Alamo, the majority of them would have raised the white flag of surrender or left the fort before the Mexican army began its assault. When major social movements of the left or the right generate a public wave, elites will grudgingly give in to some of the mass demands. What elites give up is a foot of ground as opposed to the mile mass demand. It is often said about the liberal decade of the 1960s and the conservative decade of the 1980s that those individuals who were most disappointed with Lyndon Johnson and Ronald Reagan were the liberals and conservatives whose expectations went unrealized because of elite resistance to both left and right anti-establishment calls for change. The decade of the 1980s ended with the American right's lament that people in the White House would not let "Reagan be Reagan" for his two terms in office. Part of the right's disappointment can be attributed to the fact that Candidate Reagan on the stump was not President Reagan in the Oval Office where the centrist establishment force kept the president in check from veering too far right.

Elite Sources of Power

With global elites, American elites, and Texas elites impacting greatly the course of the world, national, and state affairs, what are the sources of power allowing the few to achieve and to control things? Wealth is a good place to begin in looking at various elite power sources. "Money," as California legislator Jesse Unruh once said, "is the mother's milk of politics." In Texas, an older Mexican saying is that "No peso means no say-so" hits the center of the political mark. Throughout Texas history the wealthy have been able to use their resources to get their way. It was common for rich property owners in the Old West to have hired hands with six-guns and ropes on the boss's payroll. In modern Texas wealthy elites have let go of the hired "hands" in favor of hired "heads" with legal, fiscal, and public policy expertise that can offer multiple degrees of respectability and intellectual cover to elites pursuing their own interests in Austin and elsewhere.

If it was only a matter of income and wealth that allowed elites to buy power, then Microsoft founder Bill Gates would be the king of the world and family heiress Alice Walton would be the tallest Texan. With their net worth in the billions, Gates and Walton illustrate one source of power which *Forbes* magazine tracks each year on its world's richest list. Wealth is not the only source of power as David Rothkopf, author of *Superclass,* points out by putting the number of global elites at around 6,000 and not all of these prominent figures are covered in gold.

When addressing the question, *Who's Running America?,* Thomas Dye provides an answer that goes along with our second source of power or the holding of an official position within an institutional or organizational setting. It is Dye's view that modern elites exercise power from a lofty post within the public or private sector. His institutional elite class consists of individuals at the top of governmental and nongovernmental hierarchies. For 14 years, Governor Rick Perry was at the pinnacle of the Lone Star power system, and his governorship put him on a power plane with the likes of Texas billionaires Michael Dell, Charles Butt, and Richard Kinder. The perspective of public and private elites is orientated in a top-down fashion as opposed to the bottom-up view of the masses. For people from humble backgrounds, the ascent up the state and national political ladder can be a transforming experience with good or bad results for working people. The long rise to power for commoners Lyndon Johnson and Ronald Reagan brought the Great Society on the one hand and a social safety net full of holes on the other hand for the have-somes and the have-nots.

The Texas government elite structure consists largely of the state's two U.S. senators, the 27 statewide elected officials from the legislative, executive, and judicial branches of government, state legislators, major county officials, and big city mayors. During the first years of the twenty-first century, Texas Congressman Tom Delay wielded his version of "Hammer" power over his Republican state colleagues in Austin as he got a second legislative redistricting plan in 2003 drawn up against all political odds by using the promise of campaign cash and political intimidation to achieve his goal of more GOP House seats in Texas for President George W. Bush and the national party.

Within any political system, persons with wealth and position have two important sources of visible and invisible power. Along with wealth and position, there is a third source of power that German sociologist Max Weber has identified as charisma or the quality of the dynamic personality who can motivate and mobilize the masses for a cause larger than themselves. It was the charisma of Mahatma Ghandi and Martin Luther King Jr., men without wealth or position, who were able to transform the Indian and American societies for the betterment of all.

In Texas, charisma can be blended with fame and celebrity in today's political world to equate with what writer Molly Ivins called the "Elvis" or "It" factor. The political "It" factor exists for those who have star power and are able to transform their personal appeal into electoral and policy success. Who has "It?" In America, John Kennedy and Ronald Reagan had "It," while Jimmy Carter and Gerald Ford did not. In Texas, John Connally was full of "It," while Dolph Briscoe was "It-less." Barbara Jordan had "It," while Bill White was not "It." Texas "Its" Governor John Connally and Congresswoman Barbara Jordon accomplished much of lasting value as the former generally is regarded as the greatest twentieth century state chief executive, and the latter was seen during the Watergate era as the anti-Nixon or the ethical compass of a nation sickened by the sight of a corrupt president.

Where Are the Masses?

Much has been said so far in this chapter on "Power in Texas" about elites, the exercise of power, and the sources of power, but what about the masses or the people. Why are the many so willing to take direction from the few when it is clearly not in their economic best interests to do so? How have Texas elites been able to hypnotize the masses into supporting an economic and political system that is so unfair and unequal to working people? Elites have dominated and continue to control the masses by their ability to trumpet myths and propaganda, to hold out the "carrots" of the American dream, and to use the "sticks" of the legal system to keep the masses from straying outside the set elite lines.

To achieve mass acceptance of the elite-based structure, the few have relied first on the use of myths and propaganda to put the minds of citizens into a mold shaped around the "greatness" of Texas. Louisiana Governor Edwin Edwards once said that if Texans could suck the way they blow then they would empty the waters of the Gulf of Mexico. The presentation of myths and propaganda begins early in the public schools where the dominant political narrative revolves around the glories and blessings of the Texas free enterprise system and the freedom and liberty of democracy Lone Star style. The gap between the school version of capitalism and Texas government presented to the young and the reality of the economic and political systems is as wide as the state of Texas.

It might be understandable that elites could keep young people in the political dark as most students are interested in popularity, sports, stuff, and the opposite sex, but what about adults? Why have Texas working people so rarely questioned things or challenged authority? While schools are a main political socialization agent for youth, the process of inculcating establishment ideas and beliefs is a never-ending job throughout life. The direct and indirect brainwashing of the many by the few takes place at work, in church, and through the mass media.

For people out of school, the main message from employers, ministers, and broadcasters is to make no waves and to go with the regular flow of life. To question authority is just not the normal thing to do in Texas where things are so much better than everywhere else. Living in Texas, according to state mythology, makes a person a winner as opposed to being a loser in California or New York. In what other place in America would people tout their state with bumper stickers proclaiming "Native Texan" and "I Wasn't Born in Texas, But I Got Here as Fast as I Could." Texas pride is an intoxicating drug that causes some to lose sight of the economic and political illnesses in the state.

For Texans who can see the state forest from their neighborhood trees, how have economic elites been able to freeze so many in place denying them much in the way of upward mobility? The answer lies in looking at how elites in a political system use the "carrots" or benefits and the "sticks" or costs to keep the system working for them. The top one percent of the wealth distribution would be unable to run things its way without major support from the other parts of the population.

What strategy have the Texas have-mores used to keep the haves, the have-somes, and the have-nots from challenging their primacy in state affairs? In appealing to the upper-middle and middle-middle classes, that is the haves and the upper half of the have-somes, the one percent have-mores have delivered the carrots and benefits of professional employment, home ownership, discretionary income for travel and private schools, low taxes, and safe neighborhoods. For these predominantly white Anglos, this tradeoff is too good to pass up in a Lone Star consumer culture where new, big, expensive, and trendy determine self-worth and status.

For many Texans the fear of losing what they have keeps them from asking too many questions of those in power. Deep down white Anglos know about the misery of African-Americans, Hispanics, and blue-collar whites living in Texas. To justify in their own minds the economic injustice facing the lower have-somes and the have-nots, the haves and the upper have-somes attribute their comfortable lives to their own doing and no one else. It was hard work, an educational degree, and a never-say-die attitude that brought them the rewards of success as measured by a two-story home in the suburbs, an expensive SUV and large pick-up truck in the driveway, and a swimming pool in the backyard. To many white Anglos, the government, federal or state, had no role at all in their achieving the American dream in Texas.

Without receiving as much as a slice of the economic pie and very few carrots over the years, why have the lower have-somes and the have-nots remained so quiet and accepting of the way things are? Part of the explanation rests with the masses desire to believe in the hope for a better future. Hope in the form of superficial optimism can lead a true believer in Texas to accept about anything with a smile. Political critics of President Reagan, the commander in chief of superficial optimism, often would say that Reagan could find something good to say about a train wreck. Hope and illusory dreams keep many of the lower middle class, the working poor, and the destitute buying state lottery tickets as their one big shot for success. For others Jesus has a plan for them that will one day lead to the ultimate riches of heaven worth more than all the earthly millions.

While some people at the bottom half of the economic stratum still cling to hope, those who see no hope remain politically docile out of a sense of fear of elite "sticks" raining down on them. Through the use of state power and private resources, Texas elites have always kept the masses divided and guessing about who to hold responsible for their low standing in life. It is an unquestioned belief among the wealthy in Texas that those who do not make it in life are responsible alone for their own economic shortcomings. Looking to government for help is only met with the Reagan mantra of "The government is not the solution to your problem but it is the problem." This Reagan anti-government saying might as well be tattooed across the foreheads of elites.

While the creation of a climate of self-acceptance for economic failure can work up to a point, the few have incorporated a more active strategy of divide and conquer toward the masses that goes back to biblical times. This strategy of division allows elites to stand back and watch political in-fighting within the masses along racial, ethnic, gender, and sexual preference lines. It is black versus brown, Anglo versus Hispanic, male versus female, and straight versus gay. For the few historic occasions when the masses united under a labor or civil rights banner, the law enforcement power of the state has stood ready to kill, incarcerate, bloody, fine, or ruin the reputations of those challenging an oppressive status quo.

Has the state elite control meant no gains for working people over the years? The answer to the question is that working people in Texas have won a few rounds in the long fight against economic injustice. It was the power of Washington elites over Texas elites that brought the masses Social Security, integrated public schools, Medicare, civil rights, voting rights, and Obamacare to the Lone Star State.

When Texas working people have won policy victories in Austin, the wins have been more symbolic than substantive in nature as the upper dogs have shown their political skill in passing on to the underdogs a bus token rather than a ride in an elite limousine. During the 1990s, the political jump that the Texas establishment made from backing a white, Anglo, conservative Democratic Party to a growing white-right Republican Party was a move of political genius that has paid enormous elite dividends over the past twenty years. It is now clear to all whites, irrespective of income, that the GOP is the white people's party of Texas. Even when the Democrats nominated a 2010 gubernatorial candidate named Bill White, this white could attract only 30 plus percent of the Caucasian vote.

It would seem that many Texas whites have been infected with the same political disease of many white working people in Kansas as uncovered in Thomas Frank's book, *What's Wrong with Kansas?* It is Frank's thesis that the Republican Party has used conservative social issues or wedge issues like abortion and gays to draw support from people known as Bubbas in Texas or the white working class. The have-not vote against killing the unborn or opposing same sex marriage comes at a political price of working people generally acting against their own best economic interest whether they know this or not.

Concluding Remarks

In looking at power in Texas, it is our view that economic elites, and not the working people, reign supreme in the Lone Star State. The few display power over the many by being able to achieve their economic and political ends and by being able to maintain a rewarding state status quo. The sources of elite power come from wealth, position, and charisma. The powerful use political socialization, carrots, and sticks to keep the powerless in check. Government policies benefitting the have-somes and have-nots have come about through the actions of Washington elites often over the objections of Texas elites. To the delight of the state's upper class, the masses have been content to accept symbolic changes and small economic concessions over the years.

Works Noted

Key, Jr. V.O. 1949. *Southern Politics*. New York: Vintage.

Dahl, Robert A. 1967. *Pluralist Democracy in the United States*. Chicago: Randy McNally.

Lamare, James W. 1981. *Texas Politics: Economics, Power, and Policy*. St. Paul, MN: West Publishing.

Dye, Thomas and Harmon Zeigler. 2009. *The Irony of Democracy*. Boston: Wadsworth Cengage Learning.

Stiglitz, Joseph E. 2016. *Rewriting the Rules of the American Economy*. New York: W.W. Norton.

Neustadt, Richard. 1960. *Presidential Power*. New York: John Wiley & Sons.

Bachrach, Peter and Morton S. Baratz. 1962. "Two Faces of Power." *American Political Review*: 947-952.

Mills, C. Wright. 1959. *The Power Elite*. New York: Oxford University Press.

Rothkopf, David. 2008. *Superclass*. New York: Farrar. Straus, and Giroux.

Dye, Thomas. 2014. *Who's Running America?*. Boulder, Co.: Paradigm Publishers.

Frank, Thomas. 2004. *What's the Matter with Kansas?*. New York: Metropolitan Books.

CHAPTER TWO

CONSTITUTIONS IN TEXAS

"Humbly invoking the blessings of Almighty God, the people of the State of Texas do ordain and establish the Constitution." This sentence is the preamble or opening words of the Texas Constitution which Stefan Haag, author of the *Annotated 1876 Texas Constitution*, states is a document generally held in little regard and often reviled by just about every Texas government textbook writer. While few people would attempt to equate the brilliance of the U.S. Constitution of 1789 with the ordinariness of the 1876 Lone Star charter, there are important similarities concerning power and politics within both documents. It is always good to remember the first commandment of politics which states that elites, at all levels of government, will write the formal rules to insure and to protect their wealth and public standing.

In 1913, Harvard professor Charles Beard shook up the conventional historical wisdom about the motivation behind the work of James Madison and his fellow Founding Fathers at Philadelphia. It was Beard's thesis in *An Economic Interpretation of the Constitution of the United States* that the hands of Madison and his co-authors were directed toward preserving and protecting the propertied classes from the possible leveling influence of either the government or the masses. After Beard's bombshell hit, many establishment historians put in a great deal of intellectual effort to try to discredit this economic elite theory in the way the Roman Catholic hierarchy attacked the religious ideas of Martin Luther. It would be up to Martin Diamond in *The Founding of the Democratic Republic* to offer an academic détente between Beard and his critics by saying that the constitutional framers acted out of both political logic and economic interests.

While the motivations of James Madison and others may be debated, no such controversy exists over the political purpose behind the Texas Constitution of 1876. The main purpose of the 1876 document was to restrict forever the powers of state government. At the 1875 constitutional convention, the slogan of "Retrenchment and Reform" became the rallying cry of the Texas Grange, an organization of farmers and ranchers, which claimed nearly half of the 90 delegates as members. The Grangers and the other conventioneers were committed to the proposition of "Never Again" as they shaped a new state government based on "retrenchment" or fiscal conservatism and "reform" or extreme limits on state power. What the Austin delegates, some 75 Democrats strong, wanted to do was to erase any traces of radical Republican rule that Texans experienced during Reconstruction. To most native Southerners, Republicans were traitors and occupiers who were imposing a foreign political ideology upon the defeated Confederacy. It is on this point that Texas elites and masses saw eye-to-eye as both the haves and have-nots believed that the sooner the carpetbaggers, with their big government ideas and support for black equality, were swept out of the Lone Star State then the better life would be for all.

In February of 1876, Texas voters made up mostly of Anglo male Democrats ratified a proposed constitution that codified such political principles as weak government, spending constraints, and regressive taxation. In analyzing the 1876 election voting patterns, political scientists have pointed out the overwhelming rural area support for the proposed constitution, while city residents were casting "No" ballots. With the great majority of Texans living outside of urban areas, the "Yes" votes numbered around 70 percent to put the win into the landslide category.

This new constitution was a clear political victory for the elites of that era, large landowners and the business class, who were rejoicing at the prospects of no more Yankee imperialism in Texas. While the economic notables gained substantive benefits of a freer market system, the ordinary white males would take symbolic satisfaction from the 1876 vote as the hated Republicans and despised Negroes would soon be out of government. The new Texas would become the old Texas before the War Between the States where Democrats and white supremacy ruled over the land.

Eight Constitutions

A constitution is the highest law of the land for a nation or a state. Constitutions are legal documents laying out the political rules of the game in terms of government structure and powers and individual rights and responsibilities. From the beginning of America, the people have been governed under the authority of two national constitutions: the Articles of Confederation of 1781 and the U.S. Constitution of 1789. For the people of Texas, the constitutional experiences have been far more varied and complex as a result of the unique history of America's second-largest state. Among the 50 states, no state can match the governmental trails that Texas has followed over the years. There is no state but Texas that has been a part of a foreign country, an independent republic, a state within the Confederate States of America, and an in-out-and-in state within the United States of America.

For both America and Texas, new constitutions were proposed and ratified to signify major governmental or systemic changes.

After its military victory over England and 10 years of operating as independent and free-floating states, the original 13 colonies agreed to establish the United States of America in 1781. The first U.S. Constitution lasted only eight years as political and economic elites recognized the obvious weaknesses of the League of Friendship. In doing away with the Articles of Confederation, the 55 delegates at Philadelphia set out a new political course for America, where a strong central government would be put in place over the states. Anticipating such an outcome, the small "d" democrat Patrick Henry refused to attend the 1787 convention as this man of the masses "smelt a (elite) rat" was about to run wild over the constitutional proceedings.

While the U.S. Constitution marked a new beginning of American governance, the multiple Texas constitutions reflected a series of political starts, stops, and restarts for the people of Texas. It is interesting to note that a mild disagreement exists among historical observers over the exact number of state constitutions. The official total from the Office of the Texas Attorney General is eight. Despite the official number, many textbook authors have settled on six based on their view that Texas government life began in 1836 when Tejas won its independence from Mexico and became a republic. Starting with the 1836 document would put the number at six. To get to seven and eight means recognizing the constitutions of 1824 and 1827 when Tejas was a territory and a state within Mexico.

Given today's Tea Party Republican beliefs about building walls and self-deportation, it is sheer historical irony that it was the Anglos in the early nineteenth century who were the illegals storming into Tejas from Tennessee and other parts of the South to upset the Mexican political status quo. Along with other reasons, it probably did not help Mexico that the first two Texas constitutions established Catholicism as the state religion, made slavery illegal, and offered Spanish as the official language. What was a poor Gringo to do other than to fight for freedom from this Mexican oppression, so that an independent republic could be created where slave owners, business elites, and white males could practice their version of control over blacks, laborers, and women under the Lone Star flag.

The legal status of Texas would change in 1845 when the Republic would be admitted as the 28th state to enter the Union. As Old Glory was raised over Texas, a fourth constitution would take effect in which a government modeled along the line of other Southern states where weak government and slavery were political fixtures. The fourth Texas constitution would be replaced as state secessionist Democrats voted to leave the United States and wrote a new state constitution. The voters of Texas would approve what the convention secessionists recommended by an 85 percent approval mark at a February 23, 1861 special election. Southerners and Texans were making good on their threat to leave the U.S.A. if that "Black" Republican Abraham Lincoln should be elected president. The Confederate Constitution of 1861, Texas' fifth in history, established that the 28th U.S. state would become the seventh state to join the Confederate States of America (CSA). As a member of the C.S.A., slavery would be legal in Texas and the emancipation of slaves illegal.

With Lee's surrender to Grant in 1865, the Civil War was over for Texas and the South. What awaited the defeated states was their readmission and reconstruction into the Union at a high political price. Federal government authorities effectively wrote two Texas constitutions, which took effect in 1866 and 1869. The practical impact here was to undermine the position of Texas elites and the white masses as slavery and secession were outlawed forever under the Presidential Reconstruction Constitution of 1866. The Congressional Reconstruction Constitution of 1869, the state's seventh legal charter, would bring a strong state government imposed upon Texas elites and masses through the authority of Republican Party officeholders and the stationing of federal troops in the Lone Star State to maintain law and order.

It is worth noting that Republican officials and Yankee soldiers had the political effect of unifying elites and masses in Texas in a common bond against the Northern occupiers. Throughout American and Texas history, political and economic elites had been able to convince the white Anglo masses that killing Indians, fighting Mexicans, and enslaving African-Americans were essential to furthering the causes of Christianity and manifest destiny. It was Texas elite mastery over the masses that found whites without property supporting slavery, an institution benefitting just a few wealthy plantation owners. Why did the white masses go along with black enslavement? According to Texas historian Archie McDonald, white complicity in the cruel slave system was based on identification with white supremacy, and the hope that one day the average white man would be rich enough to own black slaves.

It is often said that the first stolen presidential election in American history was the 1876 contest between Republican Rutherford B. Hayes and Democrat Samuel Tilden. With Democrat Tilden carrying the popular vote and the Electoral College count in dispute, political party elites struck a deal to turn over the White House to Republican Hayes in exchange for the removal of federal control and U.S. soldiers from the Democratic South. This arrangement was the deal of the century for Texas Democrats who rid themselves of the likes of Republicans, in the mold of Governor Edmund Davis, and freed the Lone Star State from Washington's clutches.

With a Democratic governor in office in 1874, the way was cleared for the Texas Grange and its allies to write a new constitution in 1875 that would establish a political system of, by, and for private elites. While the masses, or ordinary folks, were overjoyed to see the Yankee troops "go home," they probably failed to appreciate the political consequences of the sale of their democratic souls to this devil of a constitution. In the future the 1876 Faustian bargain would put the people in a subservient position where private outside powers could not be checked easily by the countervailing power of the public government. There would be, to put it mildly, no weapons in the government arsenal to deter the actions of economic elites in their pursuit of financial gain.

The 1876 Constitution

From a structural and functional standpoint, how do the current American and Texas Constitutions compare? Before any comparison can be made, one should lay out the different public philosophies of the U.S. and Lone Star Founding Fathers. While the national framers accepted government as a necessary fact of life, the Texas framers saw government as an evil force that must be imprisoned to avoid any harm coming to state inhabitants. The country's constitutional fathers accepted the famous observation of James Madison that government was necessary because men were not angels. This view may have been acceptable at Philadelphia, but it made little headway at the 1875 Texas Convention where the delegates believed that government was el diablo and men could be angelic without it.

To simplify the two outlooks: the U.S. framers were pro-government in orientation, while the Texas framers held anti-government views. This difference may be as much about history as it is about philosophy. Under the Articles of Confederation, America was failing as a nation due to the federal government's inability to tax, to spend, and to raise an army. Under the Reconstruction constitutions, Texas was unrecognizable to native elites as state government was seen as too big and too intrusive for their liking in the areas of taxing, educating, and policing.

With no Aristotelian mean in sight, national elites chose more government power and state elites selected less power. Each choice made some sense given the context of eighteenth century America and nineteenth century Texas. Despite the Lone Star fathers' disagreement with their national brothers over the proper role of government in society, they did agree with them on incorporating the political principles of popular sovereignty, representative government, separation of powers, and checks and balances into a written constitution.

How do the Texas and U.S. Constitutions compare today on structural and functional grounds? In 2016, the Texas charter had 17 articles and 491 amendments while the United States document had seven articles and 27 amendments. In both constitutions, the institutional components of government: legislative, executive, and judicial departments or branches follow in the same order as Texas Articles III, IV, and V parallel U.S. Articles I, II, and III. It is clear that the state and federal framers wanted the bicameral legislatures of houses and senates to be the leading governmental branches, but here is where the similarity ends.

There is an old Texas saying, "No man's life, property, or liberty are safe while the state Legislature is in session." Perhaps the saying came about because the Texas House and Senate convene in Austin for just 140 days in regular session in odd-numbered years. The biennial legislative meetings contrast sharply with the annual meetings of the U.S. Congress. This every-other-year state feature reveals a great deal about the Grangers' government distrust in establishing a system where the "people's branch" would only sit from January-to-May the year following each state election. For twenty-first century Texas government loathers, this meant that their full-time hating could be turned to Washington for 590 days in a two-year period.

Prior to his White House days, Woodrow Wilson, the only political scientist ever to be president, wrote *Congressional Government* about the importance of a national legislature leading the way for the American people and acting as a main line of defense against tyranny. This pre-presidential Wilsonian legislative preference also was the choice of Democratic Grangers who had lived under the "tyranny" of Republican Governor Edmund Davis. To prevent another Davis in Texas, the state framers created a plural executive in the 1876 Constitution with the real government power residing with the lieutenant governor, a member of the Senate, and not the governor, a largely ceremonial figure within the executive branch.

Article IV of the Texas Constitution established a plural executive system, quite a contrast from the single executive U.S. system in which the president picks his vice-president and chooses fifteen cabinet department secretaries pending Senate confirmation. The governor has no formal control over the other members of the executive branch that include the key state Offices of Lieutenant Governor, Attorney General, Comptroller of Public Accounts, and General Land Commissioner. The Texas executive officeholders are not beholding to any governor for their authority comes from the constitution and the voters.

Within any representative democracy, the political principles of majority rule, minority rights, equality of opportunity, and the rule of law are sacred promises made to citizens. It is the judiciary that often is entrusted to uphold minority rights, be these rights related to anti-establishment speech or unpopular actions. Article III of the U.S. Constitution and Article V of the Texas Constitution lay out very different judicial systems. It is the president and senators who select all federal district, appellate, and Supreme Court judges for life terms of office. In Texas, the voters elect their state and local judges from the lowest to the highest courts for fixed office terms of four or six years.

Little doubt exists that Texas elites and some of the masses were outraged in 2012 when U.S. Supreme Court Chief Justice John Roberts cast the deciding vote to uphold the constitutionality of Obamacare. Nominated by President George W. Bush, Chief Justice Roberts felt no direct political pressure in approving "socialized medicine" for he was safe in the knowledge that Tea Party Republicans and "Fox News" viewers could not vote him out of office. Had Roberts been on the Texas Supreme Court, he would have had to face the voters in an upcoming election and explain his Benedict Arnold decision to fellow Republicans.

The U.S. and Texas Constitutions have built similar structural political systems with three branches or departments of government along with a series of checks and balances woven throughout the three. It is within the functional or operational government areas, however, in which the two constitutions present night-and-day differences. America's national charter is an open-ended essay as compared to the true-false nature of the Texas document; it is the grand Philadelphia poetry of 1789 versus the Austin prose of 1876.

The wide-open spaces of the U.S. Constitution can be appreciated by the fact that only 27 amendments have been added to the base of seven original articles. The Founding Fathers wanted to allow future generations the freedom to act or not to act in the national interest. No such freedom would be permitted at the state level where the Texas Constitution was constructed as a book of statutes with "No" being the operative word. The 1876 document resembled more the Ten Commandments of the Bible than the Eight Beatitudes of Jesus as government prohibition after government prohibition was stitched forever into the Texas legal fabric.

Political change in America over time has come about without the necessity of passing a formal constitutional amendment, but this certainly is not the case in Texas where amendments are needed to bring about all procedural changes. Formal amendments are required to free the Lone Star State from its strict nineteenth century parents who laid down the law in 1875 by saying "No" to their future offspring. This situation best explains why Texas has close to 500 amendments with even two-year textbooks unable to keep up with the exact number. To turn many of the constitutional don'ts into legal do's requires a formal amendment, and this is where Article XVII comes into play.

The state amendment process as outlined in Article XVII is straightforward and clear as opposed to the convoluted nature of the U.S. amendment procedures as detailed in Article V. As opposed to Article V's four different ways to change the national constitution, Texas Article XVII provides just one method for amending the state constitution. To change the 1876 document requires 21 senators and 100 representatives to vote "Yes" on a proposed amendment, and ratification takes place by a simple majority vote of citizens at a general or special election. In 2017 the 85th Legislature proposed seven new constitutional amendments for voter approval.

At the beginning of this chapter, suspense over how many stars professional reviewers would award the Texas Constitution was not allowed to build up as it was revealed that academics had little good to say about the 1876 charter. While the university vote is in, this judgement has not been the view of all as Houston writer Lynn Ashby wrote a newspaper column years ago, "We Rather Trust Our Constitution," in which he offered a dissenting view. It was Ashby's contention that the Texas Constitution was a list of "don'ts" that kept the state government from doing bad things to the people of Texas. His opinion stems from the position of Texans who believe that government, national or state, can do no good, and more often than not does great harm. It would appear that Ashby was sipping Texas tea before it became a main item on the Republican Party menu.

A Model State Constitution

What makes up a model state constitution? State constitutional experts, such as University of Texas professor Janice May, have written that a model constitution should be simple, brief, and understandable, while allowing the institutions of government to make public policy. It is reasonable to conclude that the Texas Constitution is neither simple nor brief nor understandable, and public policymaking is highly restricted.

The classic "Keep It Simple Stupid" doctrine applies to many things, but it cannot be connected to the current state charter.

Unlike the U.S. Constitution where articles and amendments are numbered and occupy their separate space, Texas amendments are stuffed into the constitution like dressing into a turkey. Trick Question—What is the First Amendment of the Texas Constitution? Answer—As there are no beans in Texas chili, there is not one numbered amendment in the state document. What happens to a ratified amendment is that it is jammed into the article where it would appear to fit. This marriage of new amendments to old articles makes for a complicated situation for those trying to derive meaning from the constitution.

Failing to meet the simplicity test for a model state constitution, the 1876 charter does even worse on the second measurement scale of brevity. The ideal length of a model state constitution should be around 10,000 words. The average state constitution runs four times that total, and the Texas Constitution comes in at 100,000 words or ten times the suggested number. While the U.S. Constitution has 7,591 words, the states of Indiana, Iowa, and Minnesota have constitutions around the 10,000 standard. Alabama has the dubious distinction of having the longest state constitution with over 375,000 words. It is clear that a document diet is in order for the overweight Texas Constitution if it is to get down to the 10,000 total.

Is a lengthy constitution so bad? The League of Women Voters (LWV) of Texas thinks so in that it puts the state constitution out of easy reach for generations of school children and ordinary citizens. While U.S. history and American government books have a copy of the Constitution in an appendix, no standard Texas textbook or general work has a printed version of the 1876 charter between its covers. The extreme length has meant that teachable moments have been lost in the classroom as students can only hear about the 17 articles as opposed to seeing them for themselves in print.

Along with the simplicity and brevity shortcomings, a third problem with the Texas Constitution is its lack of clarity. A "Say What" response is not out of order here. An individual's difficulty in comprehending the state constitution stems from its poor writing style and haphazard organization. In reviewing the work of another author, the novelist Truman Capote once said that he types but does not write; the same criticism could be said of the 1876 Texas typists. The writing style of the current constitution is nineteenth century legalese and twentieth century gobbledygook. A reader will need to take a break in getting to the end of a single sentence in Article IX, Section 12 that runs over two pages and 800 words. With so many additions and deletions over the years, the 1876 document has turned into a disjointed and confusing text. A glaring error occurred in 1954 when an amendment was ratified on "Minimum Salaries" which was listed as Section 61 of Article III. The mistake made by the Legislature was that a section 61 on "Workman's Compensation Insurance," already existed, so now two Section 61's would become permanent parts of the Texas Constitution until a cleanup amendment was passed years later.

In comparison to a model state constitution, the Texas Constitution has failed the simplicity, brevity, and understandability tests. It is on the fourth point allowing government institutions to make public policy that brings about the greatest academic complaints. Scholars have come down hard on the restrictive nature of the Texas Constitution as the greatest failure of the 1876 charter. Government skeptics might see this as a political smokescreen by legal and political science experts in an effort to lobby for a big government, but this is not the case. What small "d" democrats of the left, center, and the right agree upon is the idea of letting the people decide things. It is elites and establishment figures who are most troubled by mass democracy and work the hardest to stifle populism. What the Texas Constitution has accomplished for elites is that it has taken the choice away from the people over what type of government they can have.

Unlike the Founding Fathers who did not want to write a constitution frozen in time, the Texas fathers did just that by setting up a weak, fragmented, and frugal political system for the ages. The "restrict" government mindset of the 1876 framers can be seen in the state's part-time legislature, weak and plural executive system, five-tiered judiciary of separated civil and criminal courts, specific prohibitions on government spending and taxation, and low pay for elected officials.

One of the ultimate ironies of Texas politics is that a state historically opposed to government in general should have spawned nearly 5,000 units of government. Most of these legal entities are at the local government level, and it is common for a citizen to have his life affected directly by six-to-eight substate elements. If the 254 county Texas governments are thought of as the state's "dark continents," then the municipal utility districts and other special purpose districts are Texas' "lost continents." With so many governments and so little time for public scrutiny, this state of "mass" confusion only serves to benefit private elites and government insiders who know how to work the invisible system for personal gain.

The late Senator Robert Byrd, who never left home without his copy of the U.S. Constitution in his suit pocket, was the primary congressional sponsor of the 2004 federal law establishing September 17 each year as Constitution Day. While "genius" is a word commonly associated with the national framers' document, the term "fear" often is connected to the Grangers' 1875 convention product. How well have genius and fear played out over the years in terms of continued acceptance or attempted rejection of the two constitutions? National calls over the years have been sounded to convene a Washington convention to consider a single amendment, such as a balanced budget, but it is a rare occurrence when a serious suggestion is made for a third national constitution. Professor Larry Sabato offered such a suggestion in his 2007 book, *A More Perfect Constitution*, where he advanced twenty-three proposals for consideration at a twenty-first century convention.

In 2016, Governor Greg Abbott presented himself as a modern day John C. Calhoun when he wrote about the need for a national constitutional convention called by the states under their Article V authority. The purpose of the governor's convention would be to fix nine broken parts in the U.S. Constitution. Looking at Abbott's fixes makes clear that these measures would turn the historical clock back in time to a period before 1789 when the states were sovereign over the nation. While Sabato's hypothetical fixes for the Constitution fall along the lines of providing more power to the masses, the governor's proposals would lead to greater elite empowerment as if elites needed any more power in Texas or America.

If Sabato is a lone national ranger calling for a new U.S. Constitution, a chorus of voices have sung out for a new Texas Constitution dating back to an 1887 state legislative resolution. The call for a new state charter has been a constant beat over the years with a number of major efforts failing to accomplish the goal. The failures have come about from a "No vote" in 1919, a 1949 movement coming to a halt with the death of Governor Beauford Jester in office, a 1974 constitutional convention defeat by delegates, and a "No" vote in a 1975 election.

The 1974 and 1975 Reform Efforts

During the twentieth century, the most serious efforts to write a new Texas Constitution came about in 1974 and 1975. The 1974 attempt saw a full-blown convention meeting in which 181 elected state legislators met as constitutional delegates to create a ninth state charter. This convention proposed a constitution that needed the final approval of at least 121 of the 181 delegates. When the final vote was taken, the supporters of a new constitution fell three votes short of ratification.

As John Kennedy once said, "Victory has a hundred fathers, but defeat is an orphan." The political Monday morning quarterbacks have given multiple explanations for the convention loss, but the consensus view is that the right-to-work issue is the one best explanation for no new constitution in 1974. The right-to-work issue relates to business-labor or employer-employee relations. With the support of President Franklin Roosevelt and the U.S. Supreme Court in the 1930s, average citizens gained the legal right to join labor unions and to negotiate with management over wages, hours, and working conditions.

This mass victory for the common man never set well with economic elites who despised the idea of sharing power and wealth with the people without a fight. The national business counterattack against labor resulted in a major elite victory with the passage of the Taft-Hartley Act in 1947, an anti-union law passed by Congress over the veto of President Harry Truman. Taft-Hartley permitted states to pass right-to-work laws designed to keep wages down and to make union organizing difficult. What the typical person in America has a hard time understanding is the extent of elite greed over money and political control. Elites do not share willingly with others nor do they play fair when it comes to profits and power. It was the Texas establishment's attempt to drive a stake in labor's heart that killed the 1974 convention proceeding. Business interests pushed and were successful in getting a right-to-work provision included in the 1974 constitution draft.

By including right-to-work as part of a new constitution, Texas elites miscalculated the number of "yes" votes they had as liberal and labor foes had enough voting strength to deny the required two-thirds approval for passage. For many people, "right-to-work" is a misunderstood concept as this Orwellian term masks its real anti-worker intent. With "work" already in state law, the business purpose for its inclusion into a new Texas charter was to guard against any future labor movement aiming to repeal the law. Repealing a state law requires 76 House and 16 Senate votes as opposed to the 100 and 21 legislative tallies needed to add or subtract something by constitutional amendment. By raising the bar from a 50 + 1 vote to a two-thirds vote, elites hoped this would be the end of any massive unionization effort forever in the Lone Star State.

While the convention folly of 1974 might have been avoided by excluding the right-to-work provision, the state Legislature tried to save the day in 1975 by proposing eight propositions for voter acceptance at the November general election. Had the people said "yes" to all eight, a ninth constitution would have taken effect in Texas. The Legislature's backdoor effort, however, was met with both elite and mass opposition for different reasons.

When the press reported that the Austin convention had cost taxpayers $5 million, the public frustration over the delegates' debacle came to a boiling point. The $5 million price tag for "nothing" did not go over well with the average Texan who does not expect to be paid for not working. With the public angry over wasted tax dollars, elites showed little enthusiasm for the 1975 proposed amendments or defacto constitution. It was the conservative Democratic Governor Dolph Briscoe who was transformed during the convention meeting from an invisible man into a visible opposition leader in 1975 against the eight propositions. Governor Briscoe's demagoguery about a state income tax possibility and a new constitution helped opponents convince trusting Texas voters to follow the governor's advice. With the Texas chief of state saying "Vote No!," economic heavyweights, like George R. Brown, established a campaign group named the Committee to Preserve the Texas Constitution to back Briscoe in calling for citizens to reject this new charter. With mass anger and elite dollars working together, the electoral outcome was in little doubt as all eight ballot propositions lost by landslide margins.

The back-to-back defeats of a new Texas Constitution in the mid 1970s would put the issue to sleep for twenty years. Little discussion of constitutions inside or outside of Austin could be heard until State Senator John Montford floated a trial balloon constitution in 1995 that went nowhere. State Senator Bill Ratliff and Representative Rob Junell took on a more ambitious effort during the 1999 regular legislative session. The Ratliff-Junell constitution of 19,000 words with expanded state government powers died in a legislative committee without a floor vote.

Politics is often said to be about winning and losing so Who wins? and Who loses? under the current constitutional climate? Although the Grangers did not write the 1876 document to benefit big business, the clear winners today are corporate elites. With a weak state government cast in constitutional stone, elites are able to chase profits in an unregulated Texas world. To add insult to mass misery, financial interests have made it a common practice to push for new amendments that benefit private interests at the expense of the public good. It is no accident that Texas ranks high on all polls as one of the most business-friendly states in America. While the invisible hand may be working in the Lone Star State for business, the visible elite hand is present to insure that Texas ranks near the bottom of all states on quality of life issues from the environment to income inequality to health insurance to high school graduation rates.

If economic elites are today's constitution winners, then the losers are the working people of Texas. The people fare badly on economic measures that other state governments address for their citizens and even worse on matters of mass democracy. Elites and the political system under their control are hostile to the twentieth-century tools of democracy: the direct initiative, the popular referendum, and the recall election. The Texas Constitution does not provide for any of these democratic instruments that could be used to counter economic elite power in the state.

This book's approach of looking at Texas politics from a top-down or vertical perspective as opposed to the more standard left-right or horizontal view comes into focus clearly over the missing tools of direct democracy in the Lone Star State. Democracy in Texas suffers without the provisions of the citizens' initiative allowing the people to enact laws for themselves. Democracy in Texas suffers without the popular referendum permitting voters to overturn or veto state laws. Finally, democracy in Texas suffers without the recall election giving the public the right to "fire" a state official before the end of an official term. While Texas liberals, moderates, and conservatives can disagree over Barack Obama and Donald Trump, there should be little dissent among small "d" democrats over the exercise of citizen power through the initiative, referendum, and recall procedures.

Concluding Remarks

Due to its unique history, Tejas or Texas has operated under eight different constitutions. The current constitution reflects a post-Reconstruction time when rural interests and Democratic Party forces wrote a document that held government in contempt. Academic opinion of this charter is critical as legal experts state its complexity, length, obfuscation, and restrictive policymaking procedures make it far from ideal. Attempts to write a ninth constitution for Texas have failed, but the 1974 Convention effort came closest to success only to have the right-to-work issue serve as a deal breaker. Although not written to benefit corporate elites, the 1876 Constitution has turned out to be a big business blessing and a curse for small "d" democrats. The opportunity for the citizens to take back government from elites is made difficult in Texas as the modern democratic tools of initiative, referendum, and recall are missing from the state constitution. Timid Texans can view a copy of the 1876 charter by going to www.constitution.legis.state.tx.us and conquer their fears.

Works Noted

Haag, Stefan D. 2006. *Annotated 1876 Texas Constitution.* New York: Pearson-Longman.

Beard, Charles A. 1913. *An Economic Interpretation of the Constitution of the United States.* New York: MacMillan.

Diamond, Martin. 1981. *The Founding of the Democratic Republic.* Itaca, IL: F.E. Peacock Publishers.

McDonald, Archie P. 2007. *Texas: A Compact History.* Abilene, TX: State House Press.

Wilson, Woodrow. 1885. *Congressional Government.* New York: Houghton Mifflin Co.

Sabato, Larry J. 2007. *A More Perfect Constitution.* New York: Walker & Company.

CHAPTER THREE

Voting in Texas

"If you don't vote, you don't count," is an old political saying that speaks volumes about the state of American and Texas democracy. The simple act of voting is a major political move that elites understand well, while the masses fail to appreciate fully how casting a ballot can better their lives in an age of diminishing economic opportunities.

From the beginning of the American republic, the nation's elites attempted and succeeded for years in keeping the ballot out of the hands of the masses as Alexander Keyssar has pointed out in *The Right to Vote*. Elites wanted to insure that voters could do no harm to their position of wealth and standing by limiting the franchise to the have-mores and haves of society. It generally is estimated that in the first national elections less than 20 percent of the population had the right to vote. This low percentage came about by denying the vote to women, non-whites, and males without property or America's have-somes and have-nots.

Throughout the nineteenth and twentieth centuries, American and Texas elites moved in opposite directions on the issue of who should be allowed to vote in elections. While national elites were opening up polling places to many of the formerly disenfranchised masses, state elites were devising a variety of voter suppression methods to keep people of color and the poor away from the ballot box.

National Expansion of Voting Rights

Within the seven articles and first 10 amendments of the U.S. Constitution, there is no direct mention of citizen voting rights. The legal authority to determine voter eligibility and to conduct elections was granted to the states under the reserved powers of the 10th Amendment. It would be left up to the state governments to establish voting rules and guidelines for people living under their jurisdictions. Article VI of the 1876 Texas Constitution would lay out the voting rules for the people of the Lone Star State. In keeping with the negative nature of the Grangers' "can't do" constitution, the sixth article clearly indicated five classes of people prohibited from voting in Texas: the young under 21, mental incompetents, the poor on county welfare, felons, and military personnel.

Although the Founding Fathers were silent on the question of voting rights, national political elites in the future would address the voting issue by opening up the franchise to those who had been disenfranchised by the states. While Washington would be going on offense to expand voting rights, the state of Texas continued to play defense in order to keep many people from crossing the voting line.

How did national elites expand the franchise to those citizens barred from voting in America's early elections? Through the use of constitutional amendments, federal law, and Supreme Court decisions, elites employed these three methods to extend voting rights to people previously judged by the states to be unfit to vote. This national campaign for political democracy would take over 100 years to complete with Texas elites fighting a rearguard action to stop the extension of the most elementary exercise associated with a democratic system.

To expand voting rights, Congress ushered in four constitutional amendments intended to give African-Americans (15th Amendment), women (19th Amendment), the poor (23rd Amendment), and the young (26th Amendment) access to the ballot. The 15th Amendment (1870) stated that the right of the U.S. citizens to vote cannot be prevented by the nation or any state based on skin color. While national elites backed black voting rights, it would be state elites, especially in Texas, who would devise ways to effectively disenfranchise African-Americans until 1965.

While the 15th Amendment brought a Lone Star State political backlash, the 19th Amendment (1920) providing woman the right to vote brought no such resistance following its implementation. The different reaction might be seen in the perception of elite control over these two separate classes of people. For Southern elites the emancipated slaves were no longer under their lock and key. It was thought to be a different matter for married and single women who would still be perceived to be under the house control of husbands and fathers. While blacks now were independent of plantation control, women were assumed to be dependent on male economic support and political direction. It might appear to be a combination of color and control that would explain Texas elite hostility toward the extension of voting rights to blacks and the calm acceptance of voting rights for women.

With African-American and female voting rights written into constitutional amendments, the poor and the young would find the 24th Amendment (1964) and the 26th Amendment (1971) legalizing voting for them. Under the 24th Amendment, the poll tax, a fee citizens had to pay to vote, was abolished as a state practice. The 26th Amendment lowered the national voting age from 21 to 18 during the Vietnam War era. The rationale behind the 26th Amendment was that if men were old enough to die for their country then they should be old enough to vote in their nation's elections.

Along with constitutional amendments, federal law was the second method of expanding the franchise in Texas. With the 50-year celebration of the Voting Rights Act in 2015, Barack Obama said that he never would have become president without this landmark law. While the 15th Amendment gave blacks the right to vote in theory, African-Americans in practice did not achieve the vote in the South until 1965. With Washington overseeing the signup process, black registration rates in the states of the old Confederacy doubled from 25-to-50 percent in just two years. The 1965 landmark legislation led to the registration of millions of blacks and to the election of thousands of African-American candidates in formerly all-white controlled political areas.

The third national method of extending voting rights came through the rulings of the U.S. Supreme Court. While Congress can be cited for its role in creating four voting amendments and President Lyndon Johnson deserves credit for the 1965 voting law, it was the Supreme Court in Washington that completed the national triple play on expanded voting rights by its decisions in 1944 and 1964. *Smith v. Allwright* (1944) outlawed the Texas white primary that forbade blacks from voting in the Democratic Party candidate nomination process, which was the real election as November voting was a mere formality as Republicans for decades had little chance of winning a statewide race. *Reynolds v. Simms* (1964) ordered states to draw legislative voting districts based on the doctrine of "one man-one vote." This doctrine would no longer allow state legislatures to minimize the votes of the urban masses in favor of rural folks with a different governmental outlook. In Reynolds, the Supreme Court said that size legally matters and that state voting districts must have roughly equal numbers of people. The old system in some states where it took two urban residents to equal one rural dweller was in the court's opinion a violation of the equal protection clause of the 14th Amendment. Chief Justice Earl Warren described the undemocratic situation with the words, "Legislators represent people not trees or acres."

State Supression of Voting Rights

While national elites showed no fear in expanding voting rights to the black, female, poor, and young masses, Texas elites reacted to these developments as if the state had run out of oil. What worried the powers that be in Texas was that voting rights expansion might bring about a power shift in which the new voters might bring a loss of upper-class control over government. The right to vote plus free and fair elections are key elements of a democracy that mainstream Democrats and Republicans will disregard in their desire to win offices no matter the democratic costs. The 2008 Barack Obama campaign slogan of "Hope and Change" was transformed into the election reality of "Nope and the Same" when the Illinois senator went back on his word to accept public financing and spending limits in the general election. After becoming the Democratic nominee, Obama showed that he was no democrat as he became the first presidential candidate in history to reject taxpayer money and the $84.1 million ceiling for 2008. His opponent Republican John McCain did not follow suit. Politics overrode principle for Obama as it did in the careers of Texas Presidents Lyndon Johnson and George W. Bush. Both Johnson and Bush have dark election pasts over LBJ's production of phantom votes in a 1948 U.S. Senate victory, and W's 2000 White House win that came about through the purging of African-American voters from the rolls and the questionable tabulation of general election votes in Florida.

While the idea of "Let the people vote" may be a democratic article of faith for the League of Women Voters (LWV), this precept has been a heresy for the past Democratic Party establishment and the present Republican Party establishment. For old and new kingmakers, keeping people from voting who might turn out to challenge the white, Anglo wealthy control over state government has been a top political priority. In the world of party professionals and economic elites, winning is everything and what better way to insure a win than by controlling the types of voters in the election game.

What has happened in Texas is that Democrats in the past and Republicans today have used a variety of formal and informal mechanisms to deny potentially hostile voters the right to cast ballots. From the late 1870s to the late 1960s, the Texas power structure used the Democratic Party control over government to enact laws requiring citizens to register to vote, to pass literacy tests, and to pay poll taxes if they wanted a chance to mark an "X" on the ballot. The political effect of these anti-democratic actions was that the poor and uneducated in the Lone Star State would not be voting. If these measures were not enough to stop African-Americans, the most loyal supporters of the party of Lincoln from voting, then the Democratic white primary would finish the job.

From the 1920s to the 1940s, the white primary barred blacks from having any effective voting voice. The "special" Democratic primary was open to whites only as the private club status of Democratic Party membership allowed the D's to say "No" to any African-American requests to join the club. After the U.S. Supreme Court declared this charade illegal in 1944, Democrats in a few Texas counties continued to exclude blacks from voting by creating the Jaybird primary system. This pre-primary nomination election was for white voters only, whose selections would decide which candidates could run in the regular primary now open to African-Americans courtesy of the high national court. In 1953 the U.S. Supreme Court killed the Jaybird primary in *Terry v. Adams* as a further unconstitutional attempt to deny nonwhites the vote.

When it comes to voting rights, the only Texas good guys are the women of the LWV who have taken a pro-voting position no matter how the political cards might fall in terms of various individuals, parties, or groups. Texas elites successfully pushed Democrats during their dominant government years to deny the franchise to the masses, and it is today's Republicans in charge of state government who are the present suppressors of voting through their actions. The grand prize achievement of Republican voter denial was the 2013 photo identification law whose backers claimed was a protection against voter fraud. Showing a state-approved picture to vote in person was the GOP remedy for a problem that nonpartisan observers said did not exist. The practical effect of photo identification was to keep 608,000 Texas citizens, disproportionately Hispanics and blacks without driver's licenses or U.S. passports, from voting. In keeping with the Republican ability to count the voting house, the GOP sanctioned that a concealed handgun license picture ID gets a shooter into the polling place, while a college student identification card was unacceptable for voting purposes. If students trended Republican and shooters backed Democrats, Rick Perry and his party might have said "Yes" to students and "No" to shooters.

While Democrats and Republicans historically have gone back and forth on voting rights, neither party has clean democratic hands. The actions of the blues and the reds stem more from cui bono, or for whose benefit?, than any deep commitment to the democratic rules of the game. Both parties have served elite interests by playing the voter game of subtraction and addition to the electorate. While President George H. W. Bush vetoed a national voter bill in 1991 allowing new state residents and 18-year-old state natives to apply for a driver's license and to register to vote at the same time and place, President Bill Clinton would sign such a motor voter bill into law in 1993. Most political analysts felt that the law would favor Democrats over Republicans, so the two chief executives in vetoing and signing the measure were in step with the likely minus or plus effect for their respective parties.

Is Voting All That?

While hundreds of people will line up in the cold to purchase the latest Apple product, the filmmaker Woody Allen does not even own a computer. It is true that men have died for the right to vote, while one of our authors (BL) is unable to get many of his college students to register even with the offer of extra course credit. How do Texas elites and masses look at voting? For elites, voting is power which explains their desire to keep the voting population in check. For the have-somes and have-nots, the spirit of voting is a fleeting exercise with many people unable to connect the dots between voting outcomes and state policy decisions.

The question over voting turnout and its meaning follows along two lines of thought which might be called the "No Worry" school and the "Alarmist" school. Conservative commentator George Will and the late Senator Sam Ervin have been of the opinion that less is actually more when it comes to voting. In a *Newsweek* magazine column years ago, Will interpreted the nation's low-voting turn-out numbers as a sign of the people's passive consent of the U.S. political system. He noted approvingly the words of Senator Ervin about his hope that only those citizens who knew something and cared about things would vote, because everyone else's vote was just statistics and he hated statistics.

Among the world's democracies, America and Texas are lead-ing from behind which suits the "No Worry" school. Not only is the U.S. turnout near the bottom among national democracies, but Texas came in 49th among the 50 states in the 2016 election. It may be that Will and Ervin are correct in their nonvoting interpre-tation as an indication of mass status quo acceptance, but the late establishment journalist David Broder and the American Political Science Association (APSA) hold different views of the situation.

From a *Washington Post* syndicated column, Broder felt that the vanishing American voter and the empty polling booths were reasons to raise a red flag and sound the alarm of societal con-cern. His "Alarmist" school view dealt with the question of polit-ical legitimacy as his column questioned how long the nonvoting population will support a government dominated by the interests of the well connected. What alarmed Broder was an American political system where elected officials of both parties continued to deliver policy rewards to the most well-off classes with little more than a wave to the masses. This question of support is a twenty-first century dilemma for Christian church leaders as they see the pews filled with people over fifty with a third of the twenty and thirty somethings joining the secular ranks of the religious "Nones" in America.

Political scientist Seymour Martin Lipset points out in *Political Man* that state stability rests on the citizens accepting the government as legitimate, and the government delivering a measure of economic effectiveness for the people. Without legitimacy and effectiveness, most governments will become failed states. What troubled Broder about nonvoting was the legitimacy factor as he worried less about democracy than a future mass uprising of the left or the right toppling the establishment. It was a 2004 task force report of the American Political Science Association (APSA) that touched directly on Lipset's second point of system stability dealing with the masses and economic distribution.

In the year of the Kerry-Bush presidential election, a group of leading American political scientists produced a report entitled *American Democracy in an Age of Rising Inequality.* This APSA document received minimum attention in the mainstream news media, but its powerful political message would become a future rallying point for the Occupy Wall Street movement on the left and the Tea Party revolt on the right. The conclusion of the 2004 report was that elite skewing of the U.S. political system was resulting in the screwing of the average man. This theft of democracy in America from above was pulled off by the privileged few using their superior resources of wealth, organization, and access at a time when "citizens with lower and moderate incomes speak with a whisper" that falls on deaf elite ears.

The question raised in this section deals with the importance of voting. For elites it is everything, for the masses not so much. If voting is nothing as many average Texans believe, then why have state elites gone to war so often to suppress this "meaningless" exercise. What elites always thought, and Jan Leighley and

Jonathon Nagler have confirmed empirically in *Who Votes Now?*, is that the nonvoting masses are more in favor of the government taking economic actions to improve people's lives than the voting public which takes a more austere view of government action in the economy.

Many good government groups have advanced reforms to increase the voting turnout over the years only to find a wall of silence and inaction in Austin. The resistance to reforms designed to increase participation in elections comes from Lone Star elites bent on muzzling the masses in order to protect their wealth and property from any populist assault. The issue of black voting rights in Texas is a good case in point as Democratic and Republican Party leaders have traded places on the question. Democrats have gone from foes to friends over African-American political participation depending on the time period, while the GOP has been transformed from defender to attacker in the twenty-first century. It comes down to votes not color for party professionals as they have maneuvered to open or close the voting system depending on whose interests are helped or hurt.

The Texas Voting Landscape

On voting, the comedian Chris Rock once said, "They don't want you to vote. If they did, we wouldn't vote on a Tuesday." Rock's "They" are elites who rule over the voting landscape. Statistics indicate that Lone Star citizens take to voting about the way they would welcome a move to New York. In looking over twenty-first century voting percentages, Texas, as was pointed out in the last section, ranks at or near the bottom of all the states. While the League of Women Voters of Texas continues to work hard to change the state's poor voting record, the league is confronting an Anglo power structure that likes things just the way they are. Elites view the Texas voting landscape as near perfect, so they oppose the LWV's desire to increase turnout by bringing in many "new" and "first" time voters who may not support the agenda of the state powers that be.

How do the powerful survey the voting landscape of the Lone Star State? Within political science, students of voting research divide the U.S. population into two categories: the voting age population (VAP) and the voting eligible population (VEP). Using 2016 election data, Texas had a VAP of 20.7 million people with a VEP of 17.4 million. The numerical gap between the VAP and VEP is close to 3.3 million over 18 Texas residents without ballot rights. The largest group of ineligibles are the undocumented followed by state felons; this holds true for Texas and America with around six million U.S. citizens losing the right to vote due to state felony disenfranchisement laws.

While political scientists use the VAP/VEP dichotomy in their studies, elites and their campaign advisors dig more deeply into the voting landscape to unearth a more elaborate sorting of people and the franchise. Using minerals as a metaphor, political consultants tell elites to be like Olympic athletes and to go after the gold or regular voters who show up for all even-numbered year elections. In a sample of national voting records for 2006, 2008, 2010, and 2012, Harvard political scientist Stephen Ansolabehere found only 25 percent of Americans were "golden" in that they voted in all four elections. Given the low Texas voting record, it is reasonable to assume that the percentage of Lone Star gold would be a number at least five points below the national figure. A second group or silver voters can be convinced to vote in a presidential election year, but are "iffy" for voting in midterm national and state elections. There can be a fifteen percent plus difference between the turnout of voters in White House election years and in the off-year balloting numbers. When Governor George W. Bush was elected president in 2000, the Texas turnout was 43.1 percent compared to the national percentage of 51.2 percent. Two years later, the 2002 turnout figures were 27.3 percent for Texas and 34.2 percent for the nation.

If elites see regular voters as gold and casual voters as silver, unregistered persons, making up the third part of the state voting landscape, represent bronze. These bronze Texas residents make up a sizable number that exceeded four million in 2016 or about equal to the number of state presidential votes cast for the Democratic, Libertarian, and Green Party candidates combined. In winning Texas, Republican Donald Trump ended up with close to 4.7 million votes. Every two years it is the goal of good government groups, special interest groups, political parties, and campaign organizations to register the unregistered. These efforts seldom produce the desired results as registration does not mean voting, but no registration means not voting. It is the latter association between the two that keeps voter registration drives alive in the face of long odds from registering, educating, and getting citizens out to vote. The pyrite people of Texas, or the voting untouchables, are the fourth and final group consisting of undocumented residents and citizens banned from voting due to a state felony conviction.

Over the years some anti-establishment candidates have tried to win party primaries and general elections by mobilizing the silver and bronze masses to defeat elite-backed officeholders. The prospects of mass political victories using this strategy at the national and state levels are not impossible but highly unlikely. When Senator Fred Harris ran a populist campaign in 1976 to seek the Democratic presidential nomination, he ended his effort by saying that the little people were on his side, but unfortunately they were too short to reach the voting lever. It was not the height of the Harris supporters that did in the senator's campaign; his loss may be based on trying to get casual voters and the unregistered into the polling booth. Jesse Ventura is one statewide candidate who was successful in the 1998 Minnesota gubernatorial race in getting unlikely voters to the polls. It was Ventura's reaching out to silver and bronze citizens and their votes that made the difference in his defeat of two major party opponents. Political scientist Jacob Lentz's study of the Ventura upset attributes the defeat of establishment candidates to Minnesota's public campaign finance law and its Election

Day registration system. Ventura's campaign, according to Lentz, was able to attract thousands of "Dudes," white working class young males, who registered and voted for Jesse on Election Day.

The Real Majority

Richard Scammon and Ben Wattenberg wrote a modern political classic in 1970, *The Real Majority*, in which they offered campaign advice to Democrats on how they might win the White House in 1972. Scammon and Wattenberg preached a politics of moderation and centrism in advocating that Democrats nominate for president, a Goldilocks, someone who would appeal to the middle of the electorate. It was the authors' contention that to win the White House a candidate must have the support of the real majority defined as "the unyoung, the unpoor, and the unblack." This majority of middle-aged, middle-income, white citizens held the power to select America's chief executive through its turnout numbers. The position of Scammon and Wattenberg was based on demographic factors and voter registration figures with their thesis holding up until the Obama elections. Where voting America stood in the 1970s and 1980s is where Texas stands today due to state election laws and to the political custom of nonvoting.

Since 1998 the Texas majority has consisted of Anglo, older, educated, and wealthier citizens whose numbers in the state population have been on the decline, but this group continues to be the tipping point of the electorate. Real majority Texans are registered and voting in high percentages as opposed to Hispanics, the young, high school graduates, and low-income people. What Scammon and Wattenberg's work indicated in 1980 was that American voters were older and whiter and more apt to vote for Ronald Reagan was equally true for Texas in 2014 when real voters chose Greg Abbott over Wendy Davis in the governor's race.

The Texas voting landscape could hardly be better for state

elites as the real majority effect means the continuation of the political status quo with the GOP overseeing the government in Austin. Recent statewide elections show Republican candidates, both heavyweights and lightweights, receiving close to 70 percent of the vote. Although the young, Hispanics, and others not fitting the "real" model are not strong Republican voters, there should be little elite worry over the next decade or so due to the low registration and voting totals of these generally Democratic Party identifiers. The serious concern of establishment elites and Bush family Republicans is not Democrats, but Tea Party Republicans who have shown the ability to get out their vote in poor voting Texas. The 2012 U.S. Senate Republican nomination contest could be a canary in the mineshaft for economic elites as the establishment choice Lieutenant Governor David Dewhurst saw his roughly 630,000 to 480,000 vote lead over Tea Party backed Ted Cruz reverse in Cruz's favor from the first primary vote to the runoff balloting. This blow to Dewhurst and elites occurred in a span of six weeks in which 300,000 fewer voters went back to the polls from March to May.

Today's distribution of votes in the Texas landscape puts elites in a position of wanting to limit not expand the franchise. This voting environment plays into the minimum winning coalition argument in that to encourage casual voters, nonvoters, and the unregistered to become citizen voters is a risky business for cautious elites who fear that an expanded electorate might result in election losses rather than wins. The current political landscape benefits the have-mores and haves, so for now all is good for those at and near the top of the income ladder. The only future elite concern deals with the growing Hispanic population which at present is not a worry as Latino registration and turnout numbers fall around fifteen percent below Anglos.

Texas elites know that voting provides the means to elect friends to key governmental offices who will carry out their economic policy ends. The first part of the voting calculation was solved by electing friendly Democrats for over 100 years to take care of elite government chores with Republican allies becoming their Austin amigos since 1998. Past political science research did no public relations harm to elites as studies used to show that little policy difference existed between voters and nonvoters. This finding is yesterday's news, however, as the APSA report on economic inequality clearly states that the two are no longer one. On general matters of government orientation and specific views of economic redistribution, voters and nonvoters are in different camps today with elected officials siding with the more advantaged voting public than the disadvantaged nonvoting citizenry.

The future hope in Texas for a greater say for ordinary people rests with the Hispanic community. It was Willie Velasquez in the 1970s and 1980s who led a nonpartisan voter registration project to encourage Mexican-Americans to participate in the political process. Under the principle of *"Su Voto Es Su Voz"* (Your Vote is Your Voice), Valesquez and others pushed forward an effort to register, to educate, and to activate Latinos about the importance of voting and the power of the ballot.

What Willie Velasquez understood, and so many of the masses do not, is how terrified elites are over the prospect of the people electing their own community representatives into government posts. It must have seemed like the end of the political world for Anglo ranchers in Zavala County when Jose Angel Gutierrez and other Chicano candidates were elected in the 1970s to county government and school board positions. What Velasquez and Gutierrez understood was the truth of Lyndon Johnson's famous voting statement, "The vote is the most powerful instrument ever devised by man for breaking down injustice and destroying the terrible walls which imprison men because they are different from other men."

While mass political leaders have engaged in spirited voting registration drives, these drives have not gone unnoticed by elites as they have incorporated their own countermeasures to combat attempts to increase the number of registered voters and election turnout. Elite moves "to stop the vote" have their soft and hard edges with anti-vote public relations and propaganda campaigns being followed by more concrete political and legal tactics.

Underlying the "no vote" propaganda campaigns are the political realizations that voting and death are the great equalizers. No matter how rich and powerful a person is, each of us has only one vote to cast and one life to live. The public relations moves to suppress voting have come from a variety of people bent on checking the masses. Rocker Ted Nugent once called for people on welfare to be denied the vote until they got off of government support. Some in the Tea Party, such as activist Jason Phillips, believe that only property taxpayers should possess the franchise. Syndicated writer Jonah Goldberg wrote a 2014 column, "Why Lena Dunham Shouldn't Be Allowed to Vote," in which he made a case against young people voting, due to their cluelessness about the serious issues facing the nation. Goldberg's position was that knowledge came first and voting came second. In *Against Democracy*, the philosopher Jason Brennan makes an argument that America should try substituting an epistocracy, or the rule of the knowledgeable, for its current democratic voting system. Should have-mores find out about his 2016 academic musings against mass voting, it will only be a matter of time before Brennan becomes the elite man of the year.

Another way to change the voting calculus in favor of the haves deals with not taking votes away from the folks but adding to the votes of elites. Venture capitalist Tom Perkins has suggested that votes be scaled in relationship to the number of tax dollars a person pays to Washington. This idea is straight out of corporate America where voting at stockholder meetings is based on the one stock-one vote formula; an investor with 100,000 stock shares casts 100,000 votes. In a political democracy, 100,000 stock shares entitles a wealthy citizen to the same single vote as the hourly wage worker without a bank account. While the ideas of Nugent, Phillips, Goldberg, Brennan, and Perkins are unlikely to take hold, it is foolish to be too dismissive of their anti-democratic suggestions in that today's craziness can become tomorrow's convention whether the field be fashion or politics.

While some of the no-vote crowd have used the mass media to lay down a political smokescreen, the real battle to rig the vote for elites has been taking place in state capitals and federal court-rooms. The photo identification state law requirement, as found in Texas, is a tangible win for those who want to decrease voting totals. This achievement is in line with the first face of power as described in Chapter One. The real power display in Austin has been the invisible second power face or the ability to pre-vent new laws in Texas from being enacted that would encourage voter registration and increase election turnout. If Texas wanted higher turnout, the Lone Star State could follow the examples of: North Dakota with no voter registration requirement, Wisconsin with Election Day registration and voting allowed, Oregon with all voting done by mail, and New York with no photo identification required to cast a ballot. Should Texas get that old-time democracy religion, Austin could lead the nation by following the European example of declaring the first Tuesday after the first Monday in November of even-numbered years to be a state holiday allowing citizens a day off to vote and to work for the candidate or party of their choice.

Through their inaction, Texas elected officials have blocked political reforms to increase voting totals, but it was up to two Texas plaintiffs to bring the legal fight against voting rights into federal courts. The legal challenge of Texans Sue Evenwel and Edward Pflenninger was to the 1964 Supreme Court decision of *Reynolds v. Simms* with its one man-one vote doctrine. What Evenwel and Pflenninger were asking the high court to do was to replace the Reynolds doctrine with a new standard based not on people but on registered or eligible voters. If this change or something like it were ever to take hold, the winners of such a ruling, according to University of Texas law professor Joseph Fishkin, would be people living in "older, whiter, more exclusionary native-born areas" as opposed to those living in neighborhoods of immigrants and their children. The U.S. Supreme Court ruling against the two Texans' attempt to repeal Reynolds in 2016 was a clear victory for voting rights in America.

The historical effort of Texas elites to shape the electorate and to control government, first through the Democratic Party and now through the Republican Party, has been largely successful. Elites always have understood that their Achilles heel in a democracy is the "vote," which explains why the have-mores have never wanted their thumbs too far away from the voting scale. The poet Sherman Alexie once said about the wealthy and the poor in America that "Rich people who don't read are assholes and poor people who don't read are f---ed." Without books and ballots, Alexie explains the mass political predicament of the have-somes and have-nots in Texas.

Concluding Remarks

Voting is the political currency of the masses in a democracy. The national and state trends have been at cross-purposes over time as Washington has expanded the franchise, while Texas has restricted voting rights. Elites do understand that voting is important, but the masses generally have shown indifference. For the masses voting is a Catch 22 situation where people feel that the ballot makes little difference so why bother to vote, when it is only through voting that changes to the status quo are possible. The voting landscape of Texas is barren with gold voters making up a small percentage of the population. The Texas real majority of today mirrors that classic American real majority of the 1980s with older, Anglo, and well-off residents having a decided impact over election and policy outcomes. Mass voting drives to register people and to get them out to vote have shown success in targeted locales, but Texas statewide efforts have often bogged down into partisan division, elite distrust, and mass indifference.

Works Noted

Keyssar, Alexander. 2000. *The Right to Vote*. New York: Basic Books.

Lipset, Seymour Martin. 1963. *Political Man*. New York: Anchor Books.

American Political Science Association Task Force Report. 2004. *"American Democracy in an Age of Rising Inequality"*.

Lentz, Jacob. 2002. *Electing Jesse Ventura*. Boulder, Co.: Lynne Rienner Publishers.

Scammon, Richard M. and Ben J. Wattenberg. 1970. *The Real Majority*. New York: Coward-McCann.

Leighley, Jan E. and Jonathon Nager. 2014. *Who Votes Now?*. Princeton, NJ: Princeton University Press.

Gutierrez, Jose Angel. 2005. *The Making of a Civil Rights Leader*. Houston: Arte Publico Press.

Brennan, Jason. 2016. *Against Democracy*. Princeton, NJ: Princeton University Press.

CHAPTER FOUR

DEMOCRATS IN TEXAS

Before there was Columbus, there were Indians, and before there was Texas, there were Democrats. At the time of statehood in 1845, the Democratic Party already was in full control of Texas government. It would take a Civil War defeat to oust the Democrats from power as the federal government occupation of Texas and its installation of Republican Party overseers in Austin would bring a radical transformation of the state.

Following Republican Reconstruction and a new state constitution, the Democrats would begin their 100 year reign of winning every Texas governor's race from the victory of Richard Coke in 1874 through the 1974 win of Dolph Briscoe. This state executive winning streak would carry over as well into lopsided majorities in the Legislature and the judiciary. Compared to the Texas Democratic Party, the New York Yankees look like a team of historical losers.

During its long political run, the state Democrats had both economic elites and the white masses working together to keep the party in charge. The specter in Texas of the "Ugly" Republican was reason enough to keep the have-nots from voting for the GOP for generation after generation. To average folks, the notion of "Being born in Texas a Democrat, gonna die in Texas a Democrat" became a biblical verse. For a native Texan, voting Republican was considered to be a treasonous act which might bring back family ancestors from the grave.

With the masses falling in line behind the Democratic Party, state elites were quick to back and direct the party to keep its political agenda in place as if the nine years of Republican rule had never happened. It took little arm twisting to get Democrats in step with the elite desire for a post-Reconstruction Texas of low taxes, a shadow government, and the absolute right of wealth accumulation. It was not the Democratic Party that would challenge the upper dogs over their views on taxes, government, and wealth, but the Texas Populist Party of the 1890s. The Populists called for an underdog program of an expanded public school system, an eight-hour workday, government ownership of railroad and telegraph lines, and restrictions on corporate land holdings. Upon looking over the Populist Party platform, Texas elites, no doubt, were seeing red before there were Reds.

From the 1890s to the 1930s, the Texas Democratic Party leadership was unshakable in its commitment to protecting wealth, property, and states' rights. The Great Depression and Franklin Roosevelt's presidency would not only uproot the national political landscape, but these two developments would also alter the state Democratic Party. The Depression and F.D.R. would set up a battle between the conservative, Anti-New Deal and liberal, Pro-New Deal Democrats which would go on for years with the conservative majority winning most rounds of the fight until the 1980s.

Conservatives Win, Liberals Lose

From the 1930s to the 1970s, conservative Democrats were on the "right" side of state history leaving liberal Democrats on the sidelines of Texas power and government. It was the conservative commitment to white supremacy and laissez faire capitalism that marginalized liberals for decades. While racism existed among Texas elites, Democratic support of segregation was a key to keeping average whites on their political side. For elites, the separation of the races took a back seat to the role of government and its effect on money and profits.

Conservative Democrats got the support of wealthy private interests from the dominant Texas economic sectors of oil, natural gas, ranching, agriculture, construction, banking, and insurance. Democrats pushed policies and laws that kept government taxing and spending programs to a bare minimum. It was the first order of elite business that the Democratic Party prevent any state income tax on the wealthy and to stop any liberal effort to enact a Texas corporate profits tax. The powerful haves also were concerned that there should be a large supply of low wage and nonunionized workers for the benefit of present employers, and those enterprises outside the state contemplating a move to business-friendly Texas.

To keep unions out and wages down, Democrats used state laws and law enforcement officials to achieve these ends. Texas labor laws, enacted by conservative Democrats, have given business interests the upper hand over labor. From the 1930s to the 1960s, a major elite asset was the ability to use the Texas Rangers and local sheriffs as violent agents against union and community organizers demanding economic and political changes.

Despite their opposition to big government and public spending, conservative Democrats would set aside these beliefs in Washington to reward their economic benefactors back home. Congressional conservatives, like Senator Lyndon Johnson and Speaker

Sam Rayburn, fought hard to maintain oil industry tax breaks and to pave the way for the Brown and Root Construction Company to secure federal government building contracts around the globe. In Austin, conservative Democratic Lieutenant Governors Ben Barnes and Bill Hobby and House Speakers Gus Mutscher, Billy Clayton, Gib Lewis, and Pete Laney did all they could for big business by passing laws and exploiting legislative rules to enrich wealthy elites. The 2015 observation of *Houston Chronicle* business columnist Chris Tomlinson that the "corporate lobby, not the taxpayers, win in the Texas Legislature" is not "news" but historical "truth."

From the 1940s until 1978, Texas party politics was centered in the intraparty battles between conservative and liberal Democrats. Most of the victories would go to conservatives who had the twin backing of wealthy business elites and the rural masses. Liberal Democrats had the support of minorities and urban progressives, but they found themselves outspent in campaigns and outvoted at the polls. One bright liberal moment did occur in 1957 with the surprise victory of Ralph Yarborough in a special U.S. Senate election. In a multicandidate field, Yarborough's 38 percent of the vote made him the winner in a plurality election contest.

Senator Yarborough became a strong liberal voice in the upper house by supporting the anti-poverty programs of the Great Society and by being the only Southern senator to vote for every piece of civil rights legislation from 1957 to 1970. Even before the liberal Yarborough had voted on these bills, the conservative Democratic Party establishment moved to change Texas election law to require a runoff election in future special elections when the top finisher failed to receive a simple majority of the votes. What conservatives did was to rule out any future 38 percent liberal winners in a field crowded with traditional candidates. Here was a clear example of Texas elites rigging the rules to insure their desired campaign outcome, just as Democratic National Committee Chair Debbie Wasserman Schultz slanted the 2016 political field to favor Wall Street Democrat Hillary Clinton over the economic populist Bernie Sanders.

While there was no love lost between conservatives and liberal Democrats in the 1950s and 1960s, it was the inaction and action of liberals that brought about a 1961 Senate victory for Republican John Tower. Tower's win was in the special election to fill the seat vacated by newly elected Vice-President Lyndon Johnson. In a field of 71 candidates, Tower defeated conservative Democrat William Blakely in the runoff, after leading him 31.5 percent to 18.3 percent in the first voting round.

Some liberals like Maury Maverick, who had received 10.2 percent in the first election, talked about "going fishing" on the run-off Election Day, while other progressives chose to vote for the former government professor Tower over "Dollar Bill" Blakely in the hope that a Republican teacher would be an easier 1966 target for defeat than a multimillionaire conservative incumbent Democrat. In reviewing the 10,343 Tower vote victory over Blakely out of 886,901 cast votes, John Knaggs, author of *Two-Party Texas*, concluded that the first Republican senator to represent Texas in Washington in the twentieth century would not have come about without liberal "help."

Texas Democratic Party politics of the 1960s would be dominated by conservative John Connally's three gubernatorial victories. As a Lyndon Johnson protégé, conservative Connally defeated liberal Don Yarborough in 1962 and went on to win in 1964 and 1966. It was the conservative-liberal Democratic Party feud in Texas that unfortunately would bring President John Kennedy to Dallas in November of 1963 to see about mending the fences between the two party factions. This conservative-liberal Democratic divide was political and personal as one-time Democratic congressman Bob Gammage has told the story of Senator Yarborough's dismay at learning that his burial spot in the Texas State Cemetery was to be next to John Connally's plot. It was Yarborough who would pressure Gammage to trade burial places with him so that he would not be laid to eternal rest next to Connally.

During most of the 1970s, conservatives would win over liberals in party primaries with a major victory achieved by millionaire Lloyd Bentsen, a Governor Connally recruit, over the incumbent liberal Democrat Senator Ralph Yarborough. In the 1970 general election, the Democrats would win with the most conservative candidate in the race as Bentsen would best Republican Congressman George H.W. Bush. In 1972 and 1974, conservative Democrat and wealthy rancher Dolph Briscoe would defeat liberal state legislator Frances "Sissy" Farenthold in two primary races and get general election wins over Republican candidates. The many unsuccessful liberal attempts to win Democratic primary elections over conservative-backed establishment choices would end in 1978. During the 1960s and the 1970s, conservatives carried the day with economic elite support, money to burn in political campaigns, and the reliance on the votes of the white masses.

Liberals Win, but Lose

A watershed year in Texas Democratic Party history was 1978, when liberal Attorney General John Hill defeated conservative Democratic Governor Dolph Briscoe for his party's gubernatorial nomination. As the Democratic nominee for governor, Hill's overconfidence for his upcoming general election race against Republican candidate Bill Clements would match Governor Tom Dewey's certainty of a 1948 victory over President Harry Truman. So sure of winning the election, the attorney general and his wife reportedly were measuring new drapes for the governor's mansion. To the surprise of many including Hill, Clements was elected and this victory marked the first time a Democrat had lost to a Republican for governor since 1869. Clements' win was attributed to a lackluster Hill campaign, a big campaign war chest, and conservative Democratic support by voting for the GOP's man or not voting at all.

Along with John Hill's monumental defeat for a Democrat in a governor's contest, the 1978 election was significant for another reason in that it was the beginning of the white, conservative exodus from the party of Richard Coke. As liberals became more successful in winning primary elections, conservatives became more comfortable with voting for the GOP in general elections. Throughout the 1980s, these Reagan Democrats became an American political fixture as they voted for Ronald Reagan twice for president, while many continued their support for conservative Democrats at the state and local level. By the 1990s Reagan Democrats in Texas had transformed themselves into card-carrying Republicans.

The liberal Democratic situation was beginning to take on a good news-bad news quality in that liberals were starting to win important primary elections, but they were losing general elections to conservative Republican candidates. There were exceptions as moderate Attorney General Mark White would win his party's nod in 1982 and go on to defeat Republican Governor Bill Clements, only to find Clements beating Governor White for reelection in 1986. The zenith of liberal Democratic electoral success was in 1982 as progressives Ann Richards for state treasurer, Jim Hightower for agriculture commissioner, Gaury Mauro for land commissioner, and Jim Maddox for attorney general won both primary and general election victories. With the success of the liberals within the state, wealthy elites would begin their permanent move to the Republican Party.

Despite the win of Treasurer Ann Richards in the 1990 governor's race over GOP oil and natural gas man Clayton Williams, two liberal Democrats: Agriculture Commissioner Hightower and Nikki Van Hightower, running for the treasurer's seat, would lose to conservative Republicans. The win of "The Lady" over "Claytie" for the governor's position was, in truth, more a loss for Williams than a win for Richards. It is generally acknowledged that the Midland millionaire ran the worst campaign for governor in Texas history. Williams blew a 20 point lead and drove many suburban Republican women to Richards' side with his distasteful comments making light of rape, his remarks about Texas young men being serviced by Mexican prostitutes, and his refusal to shake hands with his female opponent at a public debate. Sue Tolleson-Rinehart has pointed out that voter disgust with the Richards-Williams race could be summed up by the Dallas bumper sticker that read: "I'd rather do drugs with Ann Richards than be serviced by Clayton Williams."

The 1990 defeat of incumbent Jim Hightower was an early warning sign of the beginning of the end for liberals and Democrats in Texas. GOP political consultant Karl Rove, who would become "Bush's Brain" in the future, engineered a win for Rick Perry, a former Democratic legislator turned Republican, over Hightower. Conservative Perry's move from wearing blue to sporting red would be a popular political fashion change for many onetime Democrats. The 1990 Hightower loss would be magnified in 1994 when Rove, now in Bush's corner, helped W knock off Governor Richards in her reelection bid. While many specific reasons are given for Richards' loss and Bush's win, the underlying general situation was that the Democratic Party had suffered too many white flights from its ranks to continue winning in Texas. Fleeing from the Democrats were establishment businessmen, wealthy elites, conservatives, Anglos, and evangelical Christians drawn to the Republican messages of limited government, low taxes, and social conservatism. These messages had been the conservative Democratic music of the 1950s, but were not a part of the liberal D playlist as a new century drew near.

By 1998 the political curtain had come down on Democrats in Texas as Republicans gained control of all 27 statewide elected offices. The GOP shut out of Democrats in Austin had also been the case in Washington with the two U.S. Senate positions starting in 1993. Following Senator Lloyd Bentsen's resignation to become U.S. treasury secretary, Governor Richards appointed Congressman Bob Krueger to fill the Senate post pending a special election. This special election, won by Republican Kay Bailey Hutchison, put both Senate offices in red hands where they remain today.

The hard times for Texas Democrats would continue with Republicans taking control over the state House of Representatives in 2003. The GOP hegemony over Texas government was now complete and lasting as all legislative, executive, and judicial offices were in Republican hands. What's more, of the over 60 Democrats running for statewide positions in the twenty-first century, only five have received as much as 45 percent of the total vote. These 10 percent or more defeats mean that Democrats, like Wendy Davis running for governor in 2014, were suffering losses of landslide proportions, as was the case of state Senator Davis who lost 59.3 to 38.9 to Attorney General Greg Abbott.

Texas Democrats Today

The famous Will Rogers' observation that "I belong to no organized political party—I am a Democrat" captures the twenty-first century condition of Lone Star Democrats. The state Democratic Party is an amalgam of heterogeneous individuals and social groups of outsiders in comparison to its former uniform and homogenous past self of the 1940s and 1950s. While noting its fall from power to the point of not holding a single statewide office in this century, the Democratic decline can also be tracked by looking at public opinion data on party identification support over the past 70 years. From 1952 to 2012, Texans went from indicating 66 percent support for the Democratic Party down to a figure around 37 percent. This is a massive decline for a major political party and much of this decline will be explained in Chapter Five on "Republicans in Texas."

While the Democratic Party is the minority party today in red Texas, who are today's Democrats? The party receives overwhelming support from the black and brown communities throughout Texas. African-Americans, once strong supporters of Republicans, have backed state Democrats by margins of 9-to-1 over GOP candidates since the black movement into the party of Jefferson and Jackson during the New Deal and Civil Rights eras. For Hispanics, the Democrats generally receive 60 percent or more in elections with recent trends pointing towards 70 percent due to the immigration issue.

With strong African-American and Mexican-American support, Texas Democrats also do well among groups classified as "Other" in the U.S. Census, such as Asian-Americans and Native-Americans. While the strong backing for Democrats from non-Anglo, hyphenated-Americans in Texas is impressive, the Democratic problem is that the math does not add up to statewide victories under current voting patterns. If the number of African-Americans, Mexican-Americans, and others are computed within the state V.E.P., the total falls two million short of the nine million citizen whites over 18 who vote 70 percent Republican.

In addition to being the party choice of blacks, browns, and others, Democrats do well with young voting Texans aged 18-to-34, gays, and liberals. The percentage support given to Democrats from millennials, homosexuals, and progressives is high, but their overall weight in the voting population does not tip the election scale all that much. Democrats also draw strong support from voters in the state with the least amount and greatest amount of formal education. It is the population of non-graduates and those with graduate degrees who back the blue on Election Day. Education and income generally correlate with voting turnout and partisan choice up to a point. As has been indicated, citizens without a great amount of schooling often cast a Democratic ballot as do people with incomes under $40,000. Unlike education, where the high achievers are D's, Democrats are left behind by the high-income earners who favor Republicans by substantial margins.

Residency is another political variable influencing voting behavior that divides along party lines. Democrats do well in the central city areas of Houston, San Antonio, Dallas, Austin, and El Paso. It is in the suburban rings of cities and in the rural areas where Democratic candidates and voters are hard to find. Along with where people live, political scientists have found that the religious factor has importance for understanding voting dynamics. Democrats in Texas continue to receive support from Catholics with an unintended boost from Pope Francis, a figure criticized by conservative Republicans as a Latin American socialist or a Bernie Sanders compadre. On the religious scale, Democrats are helped by the growing numbers of people viewing themselves as seculars or non-church going types. Texas seculars are increasing in the state population and their votes are going in an LBJ way.

Among the occupations and professions, Democrats do extremely well with federal, state, and local government workers and with union members in the private sector. It is also true among the super skilled that Democrats can count on university professors, trial lawyers, and those in the arts who want to keep Austin "weird."

What can be said about today's Texas Democratic voters is they are a diverse group in comparison to the homogeneity of state Republicans. If elections were won by party bandwidth alone, the Democrats would be winners going away. The problem for the state's oldest major party is that its support is a mile-wide but only a half-mile deep, while the majority GOP is shaped like a deep mine shaft with the largest demographic voter segments supporting the party of the Georges: HW, W, and P Bush by huge margins.

Where Democrats Stand

In June of 2016 state Democrats met in San Antonio at their biennial convention to introduce their general election candidates, to state their political principles, and to present their policy positions to delegates. From the words of leading Texas Democrats and party platform statements, what Democrats believe and where they stand on issues can be identified. The only caveat from political science research is that the average Democratic voter is not as liberal as the typical San Antonio party delegate or the national delegates who met in Philadelphia in July to nominate Hillary Clinton for president.

It was President Lyndon Johnson's expressed belief that government can be a positive force for good in people's lives as he and a Democratic Congress worked to build a Great Society through the creation of federal programs aimed at low and middle income Americans. Democrats today are the party of government with a commitment to the "We" side of society. On the philosophical tug of war between the values of liberty or equality, the Texas Democratic Party chooses traditional equality, and its modern day equivalent equality of opportunity, over traditional liberty, and its present day form of libertarianism.

To know a Texan, it is said that one must walk in his boots. So what type of boot marks do Democrats make on the social, economic, and public policy issues of today? On the social issue of Lesbian, Gay, Bisexual, and Transgender (LGBT) civil rights, state Democrats are strong LGBT supporters and are in agreement with the 2015 U.S. Supreme Court ruling in *Obergefell v. Hodges* that overturned the Texas ban on same sex marriage. A second social issue dividing D's and R's is abortion, and here Democrats continue to include a party platform statement supporting a woman's legal right to an abortion as established in the 1973 Supreme Court ruling in the Texas case of *Roe v. Wade*.

Along with the abortion question, capital punishment makes up the second part of the social issue of "life." Conservative humorist P.J. O'Rourke once wrote about forming a "death" political party to get votes from citizens who supported legalized abortions and state executions of prisoners. On the O'Rourke life-death dichotomy, Texas Democrats turn out to be pro-life on capital punishment. With the exception of the total life position of the Pope, who is against abortions and prisoner executions, most Texans and most Americans are half-life and half-death on these life issues depending on their liberal or conservative persuasions.

Guns are big in Texas with 1,017,618 state handgun license holders in 2016. Numbers aside, most Democrats are not as nuts about guns as Republicans, especially when it comes to the open carry state law permitting licensed owners to walk around packing pistols in holsters. The Texas Democratic Party is the party of gun control in a state that is as NRA friendly as any in the nation.

With Democrats supporting LGBT rights and same-sex marriage, backing legalized abortions and opposing capital punishment, and favoring gun control, a fourth social issue of importance is drugs. Texas D's may not be ready to follow Willie Nelson in his call for marijuana legalization, but they do support removing criminal penalties for personal use. Like drugs, gambling is a social question that finds many Democrats willing to change the status quo in support of a state constitutional amendment permitting casino gambling in Texas. It was the Democrats, led by Houston Representative Ron Wilson, who were the prime movers in getting state voters to amend the constitution in 1991 to allow a state lottery.

While taking the liberal side on social issues, state Democrats today are in liberal economic step with national Democrats as well on the fiscal issues of government taxing and spending. Texas Democrats favor progressive taxation and higher expenditures for public goods like K-16 education and infrastructure construction projects. Although the "T" word is a dirty word among conservatives, Democrats do talk of raising more revenue by targeting tax increases on big businesses as one way to up state revenues. To appreciate the difference between the present Democratic Party and its conservative past, a trip back to 1959 is an eye opener. In the year before Kennedy was elected president, the Texas Legislature, controlled by conservative Democrats, passed a state resolution requiring Congress to call a national constitutional convention for the purpose of repealing the 16th Amendment that permitted Washington to lay and collect taxes on income. Democrats today do support a higher minimum wage law for employees. They also stand with labor unions in their organizing efforts of fast food and home care workers for living wages, health care coverage, and retirement support for the many Texans trapped in the 1099 world of part-time jobs and no employment benefits. The Democratic economic philosophy is based on government playing a "hands-on" role to check and balance global capitalism and private greed from spinning out of control. It is the willingness of the blues to use state regulatory power to achieve their goal of a level playing field for the masses in a state that has always allowed wealthy elites a free reign.

Along with their social and economic stances, Texas Democrats can be distinguished from Republicans on such public policy matters as education, health care, immigration, and the environment. The state Democratic Party is the party of public education. It strongly supports increased government funding for schools and higher pay and better benefits for teachers. Texas D's backed President Obama's common core curriculum with its K-12 English and Math requirements, but they have pushed away from the strict use of standardized test results as a method of evaluating teacher performance. Few Democrats show much enthusiasm for school vouchers, home schooling, and private school charters as these education avenues are viewed as undercutting the traditional mission of local neighborhood schools by diverting tax dollars away from cash-strapped classrooms.

While Texas Democrats have not been 100 percent Obama supporters on education, their party has fully supported the 2010 Affordable Care Act (ACA). With the Lone Star State having the greatest number of uninsured adults and children in America, Democrats find no moral or political reason not to be advocates of Obamacare. Democrats have wanted Medicaid expanded under the ACA to include more low-income Texans, only to find that Governor Greg Abbott and Austin Republicans wanted no part of this expansion.

In 2012, Mitt Romney talked of self-deportation for the undocumented, and Donald Trump campaigned in 2016 on building a "great, great wall" paid for by Mexico as a solution to stopping illegal immigration. State Democrats have seen immigration differently as they have supported a clear path to citizenship for the two million unauthorized residents in Texas. Democrats back amnesty for noncitizens living in the state if they meet certain legal, tax, and language requirements. For the under 35 Dreamers, citizenship would be offered for those who have served honorably in the U.S. military or completed two years of college.

While education, health care, and immigration have been important issues in twenty-first century Texas, the environmental issue has been the one policy that has seen the greatest movement by state Democrats to the national party position. Former Republican Attorney General Greg Abbott, who once described his job as getting up in the morning, suing the EPA in the afternoon, and going home at night, reflects the state elite hostility to federal clean air standards and is much in line with Ronald Reagan's famous claim that trees cause more pollution than cars. For today's Democrats, global warming science is irrefutable. In the effort to combat adverse climate change, the state party has joined its national counterpart to support federal proposals to limit toxic chemicals in the air and water, to have higher fuel standards for vehicles, and to establish green initiatives that promote alternative energy sources.

Elitism in the Democratic Party

For much of the twentieth century, wealthy business interests controlled the Texas Democratic Party apparatus, candidate selections, and major policy positions. Significant Lone Star economic notables, like George Brown and Sid Richardson, advanced the political careers of Lyndon Johnson, Sam Rayburn, and John Connally.

In *Cronies*, Robert Bryce pointed out that Johnson, Rayburn, and Connally were big beneficiaries of corporate largesse. In the 1948 Senate election, Brown and Richardson provided airplanes to fly LBJ to campaign stops around the state. In addition to legal help brought in to assist in bringing out a favorable final vote count for Johnson, Bryce claims that corporate planes were used "to transport grocery sacks" of money to fund his campaign effort.

With business elites deserting the Democrats in the 1980s, it would appear that the Texas party would become in the words of Jules Witcover the *Party of the People*. This party of the people notion would prove to be an illusion as new elites, wealthy trial lawyers, stepped in to fill the void left by departing business elites. For rich trial lawyers, their first concern was serving their economic interests and offering lip service to the political concerns of the poor, minorities, and the working class. Famous trial lawyers make their millions by winning lawsuits on behalf of clients claiming injuries from industries and hospitals. Trial lawyers, like TV's Jim Adler, the "Hammer," and Brian Loncor, the "Strong Arm," hope court victories will add to their wealth and fame.

While trial lawyers say they care about good government and will fight for the little guy, their real goal in Austin is to repeal tort reform that became law in the 2003 Republican-controlled Legislature. Tort reform, an issue developed by Karl Rove for the GOP, was designed to strike at the bank accounts of trial lawyers, a major Democratic Party interest group. What tort reform did was to limit trial lawyers to $250,000 in non-economic cases, to put new restrictions on medical malpractice suits, and to prevent venue shopping where attorneys file their cases in the courts of friendly judges. Tort reform has cost the trial lawyers millions of dollars in legal fees, caused some lawyers to leave the state, and put some firms out of business.

In *Fat Cats and Democrats*, G. William Domhoff estimated that the role of the rich in the party of Andrew Jackson accounted for nearly half of Democratic Party campaign contributions. In Texas today, the anti-trial lawyer group Texans for Lawsuit Reform has claimed that 80 percent of campaign money for Democrats comes from trial lawyers. This claim was judged to be mostly true by "Politifact," a fact-checking organization, which put the percentage closer to 75 percent. Trial lawyers clearly are the moneymen for Texas D's. They are the Democratic puppet masters pulling the strings when it comes to candidate selection and policy positions.

Who are these wealthy party elites and how do they operate? Matt Angle, described by some as the "Democratic Party" in Texas, is a former staff member of ex-Congressman Martin Frost and controller of the Texas Democratic Party Trust. This trust puts together voter files, targets likely Democratic supporters, provides candidate research, and even pays party staff salaries. It was Dallas trial lawyer Fred Barron who created and financed this political operation.

Other major blue elites are attorneys Steve and Amber Moystn. This power couple uses their money in a shadowy way to create, according to political reporter Paul Burka, "front groups" for the purpose of providing policy legitimacy and political cover for trial lawyer money which will not show up on campaign spending reports. Cover groups, backed by the Moystns, include: Texans for Public Education, Texans for Insurance Reform, Vote Texas, First Tuesday, Texans for Public Justice, Texas Values Coalition, Back to Basics PAC, and the Lone Star Project.

A much-publicized Moystn group was Battleground Texas led by Jeremy Bird, a consultant to the 2012 Obama re-election team. Bird is a specialist on voter registration, the identification of likely supporters, and get-out-the-vote efforts. Battleground Texas did successfully register a significant number of new voters in 2013 and 2014, but unfortunately many of these registrants did not show up on Election Day as Republicans crushed Democrats like Wendy Davis and Leticia Van de Putte.

With labor unions having little money to spend on campaigns these days, trial lawyer funding has been essential to Democrats running for office. Most of these trial lawyer funded races have been light on issues that might motivate average Texans to cast a ballot for the D's as election after election show the masses missing in action when it comes to voting. If Angle, the Moystns, and Bird were executives for a major business, they probably would have been told that "you're fired" by now, but such is not the way when you own the company which is the hold trial lawyers have over the state Democratic Party. In *Listen, Liberal*, Thomas Frank recently referred to the national Democratic Party as "Liberalism for the rich." In Texas the Democratic Party has become, "Liberalism for the rich trial lawyers."

A Bright Democratic Future?

Demography is political destiny in Texas as many voting analysts have said. It is the view of many analysts that a Democratic comeback to power is just around the corner as the Hispanic population in Texas expands at an ever-increasing rate over Anglo growth. Census figures indicate that Texas today is less than 50 percent white non-Hispanic, so with the continued Hispanic population expansion and its strong Democratic affiliation it will only be a matter of time before Texas turns blue again.

The idea of an inevitable victory has influenced Democratic Party strategy in recent general elections. The party's brain trust has believed that the right mix of candidates will lead to election wins. To catch the wave of soaring minority populations, the Democrats built a dream team in 2002 to touch all three major ethnic bases to compete against the all-white Republican slate. Tony Sanchez, a wealthy Hispanic businessman who poured millions of dollars into his own campaign, headed the Democratic ticket for governor. For lieutenant governor, the Democrats picked Anglo John Sharp, a former state comptroller. The blue choice for the U.S. Senate was African-American Dallas Mayor Ron Kirk.

Democratic strategists thought that this 3-way ticket of diversity would increase minority-voting turnout with Sanchez and Kirk playing major election roles that would result in wins across the board. Turnout in 2002 did go up with Tony Sanchez increasing the Democratic vote by 650,000 more than in 1998, but the gubernatorial Democratic nominee received just 43 percent of the overall vote. The familiar record of "Democrats lose, Republicans win" first heard four years before would start to become a popular political tune in Texas as GOP sweeps of statewide offices became the norm.

In 2006 the Democratic strategy was to set aside its United Nations ticket of 2002 and to try a political flanking maneuver with the intended or unintended help of two well-known independents in an effort to beat Governor Rick Perry. Hoping that Texas gadfly Kinky Friedman, running on the campaign slogan of "How Hard Could it Be?" and State Comptroller Carole Keeton Rylander, one-time Democrat, one-time Republican, and now Independent, would siphon votes off from Perry allowing Democrat Chris Bell to win. The trial lawyers had encouraged Rylander to run, and they double-downed with trial lawyer Bell carrying the official Democratic colors. The 2006 flanking operation did hold the governor under 40 percent, but Democrat Bell came in second to Perry with 33 percent.

By 2010 the Democrats borrowed from the traditional Texas campaign bible by running a candidate who fit the historical gubernatorial mold of white, Anglo, male, businessman. Houston Mayor Bill White, a political moderate and fiscal conservative, went up against Rick Perry in the Republican's last campaign. The 2010 election went to Perry in a landslide with White getting just 42 percent.

Having run through a 2002 diversity slate, a 2006 flanking approach, a 2010 standard casting model, the Democrats in 2014 grabbed on to a rising female national political star for governor and to an experienced Latina legislator for lieutenant governor.

Wendy Davis would top the Democratic ballot after gaining coast-to-coast attention in the closing days of the 2013 legislative session by carrying out a successful filibuster that blocked a vote on a radical anti-abortion bill. Achieving near rock-star status among MSNBC watchers and thought of as "Abortion Barbie" by Fox News viewers, Davis' celebrity would be paired with State Senator Leticia Van de Putte, the Democratic lieutenant governor candidate.

With two strong women at the top of the 2014 ballot, the D's were hoping to increase support among white females and continue to build more turnout among Hispanics. A wild card for Democrats in the election was the Battleground Texas operation which intended to cast some magic for Davis and Van de Putte. This political operation set out to register one million new voters and to get them to the polls in November.

Between 2010 and 2014, 800,000 new voters did register, but registration numbers are not voting numbers, especially in Texas where voting interest is not to be confused with interest in high school and college football. When the election results were posted, it was clear that neither Wendy Davis nor Battleground Texas could come away feeling good. Davis received almost 200,000 fewer votes than Governor Ann Richards got in her loss to George W. Bush, and for Democrats, it was clear that their day had not come as Republicans pushed 60 percent wins in statewide races.

In her 2016 book, *Turning Texas Blue*, Mary Beth Rogers is optimistic that under the right circumstances Democrats can win again in Texas if they attract 65 percent support from Hispanics, 95 percent from African-Americans, and 35 percent from Anglos. After admitting that these projections are nothing new to students of Texas politics, Rogers offers ten ways to achieve these Democratic percentage goals by starting out with finding the right leader and ending up with keeping Lone Star money in Texas.

Rogers' political projections may prove prescient, but for now, some inconvenient truths may offset her blue forecast. As has been noted, Texas has gone from a one-party state controlled by conservative Democrats to a one-party state under Republican rule. Wealthy Texans and business elites were content in the past supporting Democrats as long as conservatives like John Connally controlled the party. When liberals started winning Democratic primary races, elites moved over to the Republican Party as if nothing had changed for them but their party lapel pin.

The likelihood of Democrats being competitive in Texas elections in the near future is a bad bet. It has been said that Texas is not a red state or a blue state but a nonvoting state. Since 1994 the V.A.P. in Texas has gone up by six million people with the number of registered voters increasing by five million. With the arrow pointing upward in terms of potential voters, the Democratic share of the Texas vote has fallen from 46 percent to just under 39 percent. For Democrats the trend line is going in the wrong direction.

What major problems are stopping the Democrats from getting out of their losing streak? First, Hispanics are both a solution and a problem for them. Voter turnout of Spanish-surnamed people is extremely poor, and there is little evidence that this soon will change. Hispanic low turnout figures may be more structural than cultural if some dots are connected. Of the 9.4 million Latinos in the state, only 44 percent are possible voters. From the 44 percent possible, 27 percent are without a high school degree, 28 percent earn under $30,000 annually, and 33 percent are under the age of thirty. These statistical categories, irrespective of the ethnic factor, generally spell nonvoter for most elections.

The second D problem is the white elephant in the room which is the Anglo voter, who has been the indispensable force to the Republican 20 year takeover of Texas government. Whites are 48 percent of the state population, but they contributed 63 percent of the 2014 vote. Texas political scientist Cal Jillson has written that Democrats will not be competitive in state elections with the GOP until they can attract 40 percent of the Anglo vote.

Allowing for the rare exception, Democrats lose the dollar chase to Republicans for campaign cash and dark money. Funding campaigns is a third major problem for the blues as the reds can count on strong backing from wealthy Texans and business elites. Republicans are able to raise substantially more money than Democrats for statewide and legislative candidates. It is hard for Democrats to compete in Texas when their primary sources of campaign funds come from labor unions, a declining presence in the state, and trial lawyers, who have been dealt a hit to their pocket books with state tort reform.

It could be that Democratic losing ways in Texas are not a matter of low Hispanic turnout, the Anglo love affair with the GOP, and too little campaign green, but something more basic to electoral politics which is giving people a good reason to vote Democratic. This is the position of former Land Commissioner Gary Mauro. Mauro has argued that his party must develop issues that excite and motivate voters and offer a clear alternative to the Republicans. The Mauro message has not gotten through as Democratic candidates rarely develop issues that address real voter concerns. Democrats always say they want to improve public education, but they cannot explain how to pay for the needed improvements. While raising state taxes is a losing proposition with most Texas voters, polls show that almost 70 percent of Lone Star residents support legalized casino gambling, yet Democrats fail to take the lead on this idea as a way of increasing educational funding.

With Republicans in total control of Texas government in the twenty-first century, a number of their policy decisions have had negative impacts on average citizens. The Republican-sponsored deregulation of electricity rates has resulted in some of the highest rates in the nation for parts of Texas, yet Democrats are silent. The GOP push for privatization of government services has caused corruption and waste in state agencies, and meant that big corporations have raked in state dough in service contracts, yet Democrats are silent.

In the 1980s and 1990s, Democrats rode to victory in the governor's race with Mark White and Ann Richards on the issue of improving Texas education and offering the state lottery as a way for paying for better public schools. Texas Democrats campaigned hard in the '80s and '90s for tougher regulation of electricity rates and insurance reform, and the voters responded positively. Twenty-first century Democrats have come up empty in presenting significant issues and policy answers as a way to increase their voting base and to pull moderate independents to their side.

While Rogers is optimistic for Democrats in the future and Mauro is measured in his blue enthusiasm, the authors join statistical analyst Nate Silver in looking at the Texas political map and seeing a continuation of losing years ahead. To be competitive in 2030, Silver indicates that Democrats will need to double their Hispanic support vote and to receive 30 to 35 percent of the Anglo vote. Failing to meet these marks over the next 15 years, Texas Democrats will be pushed back to 2050 when Hispanic population projections, assuming the same continued blue support, would put the D's in a position to win over the Republicans.

Concluding Remarks

For over 100 years conservative Democrats controlled Texas government. This control would be broken as liberal Democrats began defeating conservatives in primary elections in the late 1980s. After a few wins, liberal Democrats began losing to Republicans in election after election beginning in 1998. Today's Democratic Party is quite heterogeneous compared to its past homogeneity. On social, economic, and policy issues, Texas Democrats mirror the progressive positions of the national party. In trying to win the governor's office in the post-Bush era, Democrats have offered a variety of candidates and appeals only to lose each time. With the flight of business elites to the Republican Party, it was thought that party power would return to the people. This power shift never happened as wealthy trial lawyer elites have taken charge of the blues.

Like the story of Mark Twain's demise, reports of the death of the Republican Party in Texas any time soon are much exaggerated and are the wishful hopes of Democratic true believers.

Works Noted

Knaggs, John R. 1998. *Two-Party Texas.* Austin, TX: Eakin Press.

Tolleson-Rinehart, Sue and Jeannie R, Stanley. 1994. *Claytie and the Lady* Austin, TX: University of Texas Press.

Witcover, Jules. 2003. *Party of the People.* New York: Random House.

Bryce, Robert. 2004. *Cronies.* New York: Public Affairs.

Domhoff, G. William. 1972. *Fat Cats & Democrats.* Englewood Cliffs, NJ: Prentice-Hall.

Frank, Thomas, 2016. *Listen, Liberal.* New York: Metropolitan Books.

Rogers, Mary Beth. 2016. *Turning Texas Blue.* New York: St. Martin's Press.

CHAPTER FIVE

REPUBLICANS IN TEXAS

To Republicans there is nothing democratic about the Democratic Party, which is why GOP stalwarts refer to the party of Thomas Jefferson and Andrew Jackson as the "Democrat" party to the horror of wordsmiths. In a similar vein, blue stalwarts see nothing republican or representative about the white elephant party of Reagan to the dismay of independent-minded people. It is worth noting that the first Republican administration of Governor Edmund Davis of the Reconstruction era bears little resemblance to the twenty-first century red party of Governor Greg Abbott.

After the Civil War, the federal government insured that Governor Davis and his fellow Republicans in the Legislature would be in charge of state government. It was a time for the new Southern Republican governments to follow President Abraham Lincoln's lead, according to historian Harold Holzer, to bring about middle-class societies with Washington having "to clear the path" forward toward economic success for the people. Lincoln's Republican vision was in direct contrast to the Democratic aristocratic view of the antebellum South where wealthy elites ruled and controlled the lives and opportunities of the have-nots.

With the 1874 election of Governor Richard Coke, Democrats were back in charge of state government, and economic elites found that things were better with Coke in Texas as far as their interests, not mass interests, were concerned. It would be over 100 years before a second Republican, Bill Clements, would become governor of the state. The historical irony here is how much more Republican Clements resembled Democrat Coke than Republican Davis. The parallels between Clements and Coke are striking in terms of their political supporters and governmental outlooks; both had the backing of whites with means and believed that less government was best for Texas.

Democrats Lose, Republicans Win

To get to its present majority party status, Republicans had to undergo years as barely a blip on the Texas political radar screen. After Democrat Mark White beat Bill Clements in his 1978 re-election bid, the GOP was reduced to holding only one statewide office out of 30 positions. The numbers would split even at 15-15 in 1994 when George W. Bush stopped Governor Ann Richards from winning a second term. Four years later with a second Bush win, the Republicans now held all statewide offices which has continued through the 2016 election.

As was noted in Chapter Four, winning offices is one measure of party strength, but a second support measurement is party identification, and here Republican growth has been phenomenal. The numbers show the incredible GOP rise with support doubling every twenty years from 6 percent in 1952 to 14 percent in 1972 to 30 percent in 1992. It would be in 2002 when Republicans would overtake Democrats 36-35 percent in preference polls and stay ahead ever since by three or more points in most polls.

When did Republican fortunes begin to change? Some analysts argue that Republican strength began to build in the 1950s when

Texas voters supported Dwight Eisenhower for president in 1952 and 1956, but the data indicate that Texans still remained Democratic as they only crossed party lines to vote for a GOP war hero named Ike. Other political observers believe that Republican growth took hold when a little-known college professor John Tower won Lyndon Johnson's old U.S. Senate seat in a 1961 special election. As was mentioned in Chapter Four, many liberal Democrats either supported John Tower or had gone "fishing" on Election Day in the belief that a liberal Democrat could win the race in the 1966 general election. The liberals were wrong and the Tower seat has remained in Republican hands for over 55 years. Texans had shown their willingness to go Republican for Eisenhower in the 1950s, Tower in the 1960s, and Bill Clements for governor in the 1970s, but these were individual victories as opposed to a party sea change in the Lone Star State.

While the contributions of Eisenhower, Tower, and Clements to the building of a Republican majority should not be dismissed, there appear to be two factors that led to red growth in Texas. The first factor was the election of Ronald Reagan to the presidency in 1980 as the former California governor and Hollywood actor proved to be extremely popular among Texas voters. Reagan's two White House runs produced GOP support from Anglo conservatives called Reagan Democrats who began to vote not only for RR, but they slowly started voting for down ballot Republicans as well. Since Reagan's 1980 victory, no Democratic presidential candidate has carried Texas. While Reagan the man was loved by many Texans, conservative Democrats and independents warmly embraced his policies that developed into the Republican Party model in Texas of cutting taxes, shrinking government spending, and supporting economic deregulation. These issue positions along with opposing federal government authority in favor of state rights became the GOP foundation in the state and for twenty-first century America.

What Reagan, the former Democrat turned Republican, turned

out to be was the political closer for what Kevin Phillips had called *The Emerging Republican Majority*. This new majority would be built on Southern whites becoming Republicans and leading to GOP dominance of the White House for years. The Phillips' political prediction has been largely true for Southern state executive offices but less true for the American presidency. At the same time that Ronald Reagan was winning in Texas, his polar opposites, liberal Democrats, were taking over the Texas Democratic Party and winning statewide races in 1982 and 1986 with the crowning liberal achievement being Ann Richards' 1990 gubernatorial win.

Beyond Reagan, the second factor leading to Texas Republican growth can be associated with the political strategy of Karl Rove, a hall-of-fame campaign consultant. Rove pushed the GOP to field a full slate of candidates from the courthouse to the statehouse to take advantage of the white conservative flight from the Democratic Party. Despite the liberal Richards' victory, Republicans won two major Texas offices for the first time in history in 1990 with voters selecting Rick Perry as agriculture commissioner and Kay Bailey Hutchinson as state treasurer. With these two big wins, the GOP was on its way to political domination. By the time George W. Bush was re-elected as governor in 1998, all state offices were in Republican hands as well as the Texas Senate. The Texas House would stay with the Democrats for four more years until it fell to Republicans in 2002. The game now was over for the Democrats and very much on for the Republicans.

Moderates Lose, Extremists Win

The Texas Republican model starts with the goal of cutting taxes and reducing state spending. This model flies in the face of the fact that Texas has always had among the lowest taxes in the U.S., and state government spending for most programs is among the lowest in the nation. Republicans have also pushed for economic deregulation and the privatization of public programs and services. From the Perry years to today, the GOP has strongly wrapped itself around the 10th Amendment in its opposition to federal authority, even viewing Washington as an enemy because of its interference with state matters and private sector commerce.

When George W. Bush was elected governor in 1994, he faced a Democratic majority in the state Legislature. His political skills showed as he made friends with powerful Democratic leaders like Lieutenant Governor Bob Bullock and House Speaker Pete Laney. W's courtship of Bullock and Laney paid off as the three worked together to advance most of the Bush agenda. In 1997 the Republican governor negotiated with Democrats to pass many of his own agenda items. Bush was able to get the Senate and the House to approve a huge property tax cut, a business tax cut, a limit on abortion rights, and welfare reform. To get legislative approval of his items, the governor cooperated with Democrats in Austin to sign their bills. Bush agreed to establish the Children's Health Insurance Program (CHIP), to remove the sales tax on over the counter drugs, to create a sales tax holiday in August, to increase public school funding, and to agree to a significant teacher pay raise.

With Governor Bush in the White House in 2003, his moderation or working with Democrats was coming to an end as Republicans had Rick Perry and other party members controlling the executive branch. The GOP now had majorities in both houses of the Legislature, and red judges were elected to the state's two highest courts. Without any real need for Democratic votes, Republicans in Austin pushed a very conservative policy agenda that included: cutting taxes, trimming CHIP spending, deregulating college tuition rates, cutting public education spending, and passing tort reform.

With Democrats in the minority in the Legislature, Republican conservativism or establishment right policies were not under fire from the blues, but were challenged from within the red ranks after the GOP election sweep. In 2010 far right Tea Party Republicans defeated over 20 incumbent Democrats and increased their party's majorities in the House and Senate to almost two-thirds of the membership. Democrats now were politically dead in Austin as a braking force on right wing extremism. With Democrats no longer a factor, Republicans like Speaker Joe Straus and like-minded establishment conservatives were the only opposition to the Tea Party agenda.

Under challenge himself from House tea partiers for his re-election as speaker, Straus was no profile in courage as he watched while extremism prevailed over moderation. The 2011 legislative session brought significant public education spending cuts that critics argued only crippled schooling in Texas that already lagged far behind other states in educational performance. Republicans also made a point of supporting many anti-federal policies by suing Washington agencies and pushing anti-abortion, anti-gay, anti-gun control, and anti-climate change legislation.

By 2014 the Tea Party revolution from within the GOP ranks was nearly complete. The invasion of the party snatchers brought victories as tea-backed primary candidates won every statewide executive office but one. The party of Bush in the Lone Star State was now the party of Cruz as Gregg Abbott for governor, Dan Patrick for lieutenant governor, Ken Paxton for attorney general, Glenn Hegar for comptroller of public accounts, and Sid Miller for agriculture commissioner won victories over a Bush-like group of business conservatives. The only Republican to block a total Tea Party take-over was George P. Bush, son of Jeb, grandson of H.W., and nephew of W., who took the party nomination for land commissioner.

Texas Republicans Today

Who are today's Republican voters who keep the state so safely in red hands? From a racial and ethnic standpoint, GOP supporters are white and Anglo. In a masterful display of doublespeak, Senator Phil Gramm at the 2002 state party convention charged the Democrats with trying to divide Texas by race and ethnicity in their appeal to people of color and Hispanics. When the cameras pan a Democratic convention, it looks like a United Nations gathering as opposed to GOP party meetings where sunglasses are needed due to all the white glare. Along with close to 70 percent election support from whites and Anglos, Republicans can rely on the votes of college graduates in Texas making up 25 percent of the adult population. There is a strong relationship between the median-income line and going red for citizens earning above the median amount. The stereotypes of rich Republicans and poor Democrats have some measure of statistical validity. In 2004 President George W. Bush received 62 percent support from voters making over $200,000 and just 36 percent for the under $15,000 income earners.

From a residency standpoint, the GOP owns most of the 254 counties in the state. Suburban counties like Montgomery, north of Houston, and Collin, in suburban Dallas, push the red vote to over 70 percent. In 1994 George W. Bush carried 189 counties in his win over Governor Ann Richards, and this Republican victory pattern has been true over following election cycles. It is only in the urban counties and the Rio Grande Valley where Republicans have not done well.

Since the 1980s a major political trend advantageous to Texas Republican candidates has been the rise of the evangelical Christian movement as a major voting force in national and state elections. It was the political astuteness of the Reverend Jerry Falwell, creator of the Moral Majority in 1979, and televangelist Pat Robertson, founder of the Christian Broadcasting Network in 1977, that encouraged born-again citizens to coalesce into a political army for Jesus and the GOP. This movement predated George W. Bush's acceptance of Jesus Christ as his personal savior and his transformation from mainline Protestant into the ranks of the born-again.

Along with evangelicals, Republicans do well with the aging baby boom generation born from 1946-1964. Liberal in their youth, many boomers today have become conservative and Republican as they moved into their sixties. Other GOP support groups can be found within the professional ranks of the corporate world and among small business owners. It is expected that Republicans will carry the votes of public employees in law enforcement and the military. The military vote is no small number as active duty personnel in the Lone Star State are around 400,000, not counting the thousands of Defense Department civilian employees and some estimated 50,000 retirees living in Texas.

One economic trend in the early 1980s that legitimized Republicans in the state was the corporate relocation moves from the Snowbelt to the Sunbelt to take advantage of the Texas business-friendly environment. These economic go-go years saw Northern companies sending white collar Republican managers down South in droves, while the blue collar unionized Democratic workers stayed back home in the North. In addition to relocated Republicans, it would be the election of Ronald Reagan, a former New Dealer and union president, that would establish the GOP brand in Texas. It would be candidate Reagan who would tell America that the Democratic Party had left him and not the reverse. The actions of U.S. corporations and RR would do much to bring about a newfound sense of pride and purpose to those who openly espoused the once hated party of Reconstruction.

Where Republicans Stand

For Texas Republicans it is long past time to slay the beast, which is the federal government. Nothing gets GOP loyalists more red in the face than to think of former President Barack Obama and the "tyranny" in Washington. Past and present party leaders: Tom Delay, Rick Perry, Dan Patrick, and Greg Abbott have called for the elimination of any number of federal departments, such as Energy, Education, and Commerce, and national agencies, like the Internal Revenue Service, the Environmental Protection Agency, the Corporation for Public Broadcasting, and the National Endowments for the Arts and for the Humanities. While these bureaucratic units still stand in 2017, many Texas Republicans agree in sentiment with former Governor Rick Perry who has written about being *Fed Up* with the national government and maybe secession should be more than a discussion point. Perry's hint at separation is political red meat for the GOP delegate crowd, but average Republican voters are "Mad as Hell" about government and elect government haters to state offices, where they can keep public power in check as private power goes unchecked.

Back in the 1950s and 1960s, many American political scientists advocated the doctrine of responsible party government as a remedy for the shortcomings of the U.S. political system. This doctrine was based on two clear party policy choices combined with unified voting patterns displayed by elected Republicans and Democrats. It would take decades for a semblance of this doctrine to arrive, but many academics today do not like its results of party fracture, political intolerance, and government dysfunction. It is in the Lone Star State where a unified Republican front offers voters the "me" not the "we," property rights not civil rights, state rights not federal authority, and free market capitalism not social democracy.

When Hillary Clinton published *It Takes a Village*, a book about the need for the entire community to help in raising a healthy child, the Texas Republican reaction was to dismiss the Clinton work as socialism and an attack on the nuclear family. If you were to add the GOP belief in the Washington war on religious freedom to its disdain of Hillary's communitarianism, some of the Texas GOP philosophy would start to come into focus. To get a clear view of state Republicanism, we will do as we did with the Democrats in the last chapter by sorting out some of the GOP social, economic, and public policy positions from party leaders' pronouncements and 2016 convention platform statements. Many of the social positions of the majority party in Texas align with Christian fundamentalism. As Lieutenant Governor Dan Patrick once described himself as a "Christian first, a conservative second, and a Republican third," this personal depiction would fit many other GOP officials in Austin as well.

One social position that puts Republicans at odds with the U.S. Supreme Court is same-sex marriage. In 2016 the state GOP defined marriage as "a God-ordained, legal and moral commitment between one natural man and one natural woman." Despite the high court's *Obergefell v. Hodges* decision permitting same-sex marriages, Republicans view marriage as a lifelong commitment between Adam and Eve, and not Adam and Steve.

The conservative Christian fundamentalist view on the life issues of abortion and the death penalty officially is where Austin reds are today. A 2013 Texas law, later overturned by the U.S. Supreme Court, meant Texas at the time had the most restrictive anti-abortion policy in the nation. While the GOP still holds out hope to abolish all abortions or "killing" babies, it stands firmly behind the death penalty in the biblical sense of an eye-for-an-eye for those committing heinous crimes. Among the 31 American capital punishment states, Texas, since 1976, is the number one killer of prisoners with over 500 executions.

As a social issue, Lesbian, Gay, Bisexual, and Transgender (LGBT) questions came to center stage at the 2016 Dallas Republican Convention with delegates being strongly opposed to the

Obama administration's actions for transgender civil rights. Houston Republicans and fundamentalist ministers had led the way in 2015 to defeat the Houston Equal Rights Ordinance applying to transgender people for the nation's fourth largest city. The ordinance opponents raised public fears in television commercials about male sexual predators using women's bathrooms to molest little girls. Despite corporate opposition, this bathroom bill issue would be a top 2017 state legislative priority for Lieutenant Governor Dan Patrick as he wanted transgenders to use the restroom corresponding to their birth gender.

Social issues do carry weight with voters, and national Republicans have been more effective at using symbolic imagery than Democrats. In 1972 the GOP branded Senator George McGovern, the Democratic presidential nominee, as the candidate of the despised three "A's." The GOP implied that McGovern was: for amnesty (for Vietnam war evaders), for acid (for legalizing all drugs), and for abortion (for killing babies). In 2004 the Bush presidential campaign team characterized Senator John Kerry, the blue party choice, as the candidate of the hated four "G's." The President's men wanted the American people to know that a Kerry vote was a vote: for gays (the undermining of traditional male and female societal roles), for grizzlies (the equating of animal rights with human rights), against God (the calling for secular humanism in Christian America), and against guns (the disarming of the people by government).

In Texas Republicans are nuts about guns and believe in an expansive view of the Second Amendment. The state GOP views the right to bear arms not only a constitutional right, but as a God-given right not to be infringed by either Washington or Austin. Following the U.S. Supreme Court's 2008 Heller ruling on guns, in which the court for the first time in history affirmed that an individual has a right to possess a firearm for a lawful purpose like self-defense, weapons proponents have wanted to take this right even further. The next pro-gun goal is to achieve "constitutional carry" or the right of people to legally carry handguns in Texas without needing any state approval.

While the Christian conservative view prevails for Republicans on social issues in their being against same-sex marriage, against abortion, for capital punishment, against LGBT rights, and against gun control, the GOP is in step with evangelicals on two other noneconomic issues: drugs and gambling. With the exception of some libertarian Republicans, the majority of party members are not enthusiastic about the legalization of marijuana and other drugs and are not in favor of lawful casino gambling or sports betting in the Lone Star State.

On economic issues, many of today's Democrats long for the Roosevelt years, while Republicans now look back fondly on the Reagan days. For Texas Republicans Ronald Reagan is a bigger hero than John Wayne. What Reagan means to many in the GOP is the recognition that private enterprise is part and parcel of American exceptionalism and Texas uniqueness. It is the sworn duty of the majority party to fight against the mixed capitalism of the federal system and the creeping socialism of New York and California.

Texas Republicans are economic surgeons in that they want to cut out government taxes, government spending, and government regulations. The GOP believes in Reaganomics or supply-side capitalism based on the theory of tax cuts fueling economic growth and prosperity for all. Supply-siders say that government spends too much money and enacts too many regulations resulting in economic harm.

While some blue state Republicans will tolerate social welfarism and unionization, this is not the case with Texas reds. Welfare represents dependency and goes against the Texas spirit of rugged individualism. The federal minimum wage law, according to the 2016 convention platform, needs to be repealed as does the Davis-Bacon prevailing wage law that sets worker pay rates on federal construction projects in the state.

Since 1947 Texas has been a right-to-work or anti-union state.

Both past Democratic elites and present Republican elites have opposed workers joining unions. To this end, elites have been successful with just 4.5 percent of Texas workers, according to the Bureau of Labor Statistics, being unionized in 2015. The GOP worry about unions in Texas has little to do with the private sector and everything to do with the public sector. The red concern comes from the increased union membership among government employees, which is one of the few growth areas of the labor movement. It is for this reason that the state GOP went on record in 2016 against allowing government entities from continuing the practice of letting public employees deduct union dues automatically from their paychecks. Should this become Texas law, its likely effect would be to cost unions a loss in membership by making the collecting of dues a more difficult process.

With the Democrats being the party of public education and school teachers, Republicans have embraced the mantle as the champions of parental school choice, the traditional curriculum of the three R's of reading, writing, and arithmetic, and of teacher and school accountability. Just as the GOP sees competition as the savior of the economic system, competition can make a stronger Texas educational system. In the field of higher education, the red party may be moving to get out front with voters on questions of college tuition costs, faculty teaching workloads, university research value, and lifetime tenure employment for professors. The Republicans will gladly leave the student debt issue to the Democrats.

When it comes to the U.S. Department of Education and to affirmative action college admissions programs, the GOP shouts, "No," to these two national Democratic monstrosities. The Texas reds yell, "Hell No," when it comes to the Obamacare health system. If Republicans continue to believe in the unconstitutionality and unworthiness of the ACA, what is the GOP alternative to Obama's illegitimate baby? The Texas Republican answer to the medical care question is to go back to a free market based health system. It is through competition, transparency, limited malpractice awards, private health savings accounts, and personal wellness responsibility that will mean a better policy outcome for the Lone Star State than the health system of Obamacare and the Veterans Administration.

For a border state like Texas, the immigration issue is a major concern, and the GOP view of the issue deals with state security and federal law enforcement. Among Republican officials in Austin, many would be counted among the ranks of Trump's wall builders. The Republican view of immigration seldom strays from such fear factors as drugs, violence, and terrorism. With Washington's failure to keep illegals out of Texas, the 2016 party platform called for the Lone Star State to enter into a security pact with neighboring states to enforce U.S. immigration law. If the Department of Homeland Security will not do its job, perhaps the Texas Rangers and private citizens should be given a try. The past moderate stance of Governor George W. Bush on immigration is seen as a mistake and too much like Obama amnesty to many in the Republican Party today.

Despite the twenty-first century view of a diversified Texas economy, oil is still "all" in state politics. The split between the economy and the environment is not as much a zero sum game in national politics today as a generation ago, but for state Republicans, the zero sum game between the two has not changed. The 2008 Sarah Palin chant of "Drill, Baby, Drill" remains popular today within Texas energy corridors and on the floors of the House and Senate in Austin. For many GOP loyalists, the environmental issue is less about global warming and climate change and more about pseudo-science leading to needless regulations and lost profits.

In looking over at the Democrats and their environmental views, state Republicans have just one word, "Crazy," to describe their government-based ecological measures as just so "Left Coast." For the state GOP, development comes first and the environment second. What prompts this red priority choice is the firm belief that much of what ecologists say about the earth and the future of mankind on the planet have less to do with science and more to do with a hidden political agenda bent on destroying capitalism.

Elitism in the Republican Party

The elite domination of state government has been the historic Texas political pattern. Because elites have but one guiding principle which is to get and to keep power, it should come as no surprise that in the 1980s business elites began to desert the Democratic Party. The elite flight from supporting Democrats to backing Republicans had its basis in the political calculation that the party of John Connally was becoming too liberal and its reign over state government could be coming to an end.

At the national level, corporate elites and Wall Street investors have had no problem over the years in supporting business Democrats, like Bill Clinton, but they wanted no part of liberal blues like George McGovern. With Texas liberals beginning to get the upper hand over conservatives in the 1980s, business leaders decided it was better to switch to the Republican side than to fight on the side of conservatives against the growing liberal ranks inside the Democratic Party.

For economic elites, Republican George W. Bush became the dream political candidate in 1994. It became even better for the wealthy backers of Bush that he started his campaign as an underdog to the popular Governor Ann Richards in a race that Barbara Bush thought her son could not win. With W as governor, top corporate leaders strengthened their ties with the GOP which now became the dominant state political party.

One of Governor Bush's strongest supporters was Richard Rainwater, an investor and fund manager. The close relationship between Rainwater and Bush brought comments from top Democrats that Rainwater owned Bush. This claim of ownership was made by Ann Richards, and it was echoed by Jim Hightower who said that the Republican governor did not make a move without first checking with his good friend Rainwater. Even if some healthy skepticism might be in order here about Democratic comments, a reciprocity of sorts did appear to exist between the two political allies.

After Bush was in office, Rainwater secured several big state deals that made him millions. As the governor pushed for the privatization of state services, business leaders, like Rainwater, gained a number of lucrative state contracts often without competitive bidding. In 1995, the Legislature passed a Patient Protection Act (PPA) to safeguard patient rights against health maintenance organizations and health insurance companies. The 1995 PPA had broad bipartisan support with only one dissenting state senator and seven House members in opposition, but the bill did not become law. Why did the bill fail? The reason the law never came about was that HMO and health insurance interests said, "No," and they had a partner in George Bush whose executive veto killed the consumer friendly but industry hostile proposal. The governor had few Republican allies on the PPA vote, but members of his party would be with W on his huge tax cuts for big business and wealthy property owners during his first term.

Bush's strong beliefs in economic deregulation brought about a substantial reduction in Texas government rules over businesses, and his actions only strengthened the ties between the Republican Party and corporations and companies. In 1999 Governor Bush made a big push for electricity rate deregulation, an idea brought to the Legislature by Enron chief executive officer Ken Lay, a longtime Bush family friend. Lay, a major political supporter in the past of both George Bushes and the Republican Party, had given millions during the decade of the 1990s to GOP candidates and the party.

Affectionately known as "Kenny Boy" to the Bush family, Lay's name would be etched forever in the business hall of shame for the Enron scandal is seen as one of the biggest corporate frauds in American history. The collapse of the energy company brought devastating human losses in jobs, income, and life savings for thousands of Texans. It was the sheer greed of Lay and his top managers that brought about in 2001 the biggest bankruptcy in American history until the fall of WorldCom a year later. Following the famous perp walk of Lay, filmed by Houston TV stations, Governor Bush would distance himself from the former CEO by saying that he was a political acquaintance but not a personal friend.

Friend or not, the Lay suggestion about electricity deregulation was supported by Governor Bush in 1999 at a time when Texas had the lowest electrical rates in the U.S. Deregulation advocates claimed that removing set government prices would lead to more competition among energy providers resulting in even lower bills for customers. When the deregulation bill came before the Texas House State Affairs Committee, several Democrats proposed amendments to protect consumers and to prevent job losses for union workers employed by electric companies. The big electric providers were livid over these amendments.

When the governor learned of these Democratic proposals, he sent his legislative director Terrall Smith to the House committee hearing where he corralled the GOP members on State Affairs into a backroom to learn of Bush's marching orders to kill the amendments. When Smith failed to stop the committee bill, W attempted to water down the Democratic amendments on the floor. Democrats may have been able to stall the Bush effort, but in the end, Texas would open up competitive markets for cities embracing electricity deregulation like Houston as opposed to San Antonio with its municipally-owned regulated utility. This deregulation that began in 2002, has been a costly misadventure for residents in unregulated Houston where consumers in 2015 paid 15 percent higher rates than San Antonio residents. As the *Houston Chronicle* editorialized, "It's time to re-regulate electricity."

It is clear that economic elites have run things in Texas, as historian George Norris Green, author of *The Establishment in Texas Politics*, has written about in his book on the primitive phase of elite rule in the state from 1938-1957. When looking at this time, Green names "names" of the economic notables and groups making up a state plutocracy of Anglo businessmen, oilmen, bankers, and lawyers. The primitive years are history, but who are today's Texas elites and what are their institutional connections? With the few exceptions of trial lawyers, labor unions, and some wealthy liberals identifying with the Democratic Party, the vast majority of elite individuals and major institutions are on the Republican Party side.

Three of the biggest elite figures backing Republicans, home-builder Bob Perry, energy powerhouse Harold Simmons, and construction mogul Leo Linbeck, recently passed away. While for years these three fat cat Republicans were some of the most visible donors to the state GOP, plenty more wealthy contributors remain to support red candidates and causes. In looking over the top individual and institutional funders of the Texas Republican Party today, the list reads like a who's who of the Lone Star State. The oil and gas, real estate, and financial investing economic sectors "go red" on a regular basis. Texas black gold giants in the H.L. Hunt family, T. Boone Pickens, the Sid Richardson family, Clayton Williams, and Tim Dunn have contributed millions to conservative Republicans and right wing causes. For real estate kings Ned Holmes and Harlan Crow, money is no object when it comes to Greg Abbott and Ted Cruz. Financiers Sam Wyly, a moneyman for the Bush men, and L.E. Simmons, who was the national finance chair of Mitt Romney's 2008 presidential campaign, have been heavy GOP hitters over the years. Among Texas billionaires, Bob McNair, Richard Kinder, Drayton McLane, Charles Butts, and Tilman Fertitta have showered campaign contributions down on state and local Republicans running for office.

Institutional support for the GOP in Texas comes from a variety of executives in many fields and the political action committees associated with these sectors of the state economy. In the health care area, the Texas Medical Association, the Texas Hospital Association, and various pharmaceutical firms, many particularly close to Governor Rick Perry in the past, all have been kind to Republicans with endorsements and campaign contributions. Communication giant AT&T and insurance companies State Farm, Allstate, and Farmers are in the red corner. The Williams Brothers Construction Company, the largest recipient of state highway contracts, and the Associated Builders and Contractors (ABC), an anti-labor organization often thought of as the anti-AFL-CIO, can be counted on to do all they can to keep Texas red. If you throw in the Texas Association of Business and electrical utilities TXU and CenterPoint, Democrats are facing a concentration of wealth and power on the Republican side that is formidable.

By 2018 the Republican Party control of state offices will have reached the 20 year mark. With apologies to Democratic true believers, there appears to be no end in sight to the GOP dominance of Texas government for at least five reasons. First, Texas in the past, the present, and the future has been, is, and will be conservative in a philosophical way with its emphasis on individualism and traditionalism. Conservative Democrats ran the state political show for decades with liberals and Republicans looking on from the sidelines. For nearly 20 years now, conservative Republicans have been the government winners with liberals and Democrats coming out as losers. The transfer of party state control from Democrats to Republicans has not meant much to economic elites as the ideology of conservative blues and reds fits in well with elite preferences for low taxes, few public services, free enterprise, and an anti-federal outlook. With the 2016 decision of the United Kingdom voters to support Brexit, past Republican talk of secession may be revised into a call for Texit from Washington in the future.

While California legislator Jesse Unruh referred to money as "the mother's milk of politics," Travis County District Attorney Ronnie Earle once called cash "the devil's brew of democracy." Mother's milk or devil's brew, money generally means victory in political campaigns, and here is the second reason for the GOP's first place finishes in Texas races. Because of strong corporate support for the Republican Party, its candidates have been able to outspend Democrats in most elections. One major exception to this red spending advantage was the 2002 gubernatorial race between Tony Sanchez and Governor Rick Perry. Drawing on his personal millions, Sanchez outspent Perry by close to $50 million dollars in suffering an 18-point loss to the governor. More money may not mean victory every time in an election, but in national contests, political candidates who outspend their opponents have a 92 percent chance of victory. For 2014 in Texas, Republicans spent a total of $265,499,961 compared to $68,197,684 for the Democrats, and the results were overwhelmingly in their favor.

Along with the state conservative ideology and the GOP financial advantage over Democrats, the third reason for Texas being one-party red has to do with the strong support Republicans receive from voters outside the six largest cities. Among the big six, Houston, San Antonio, Dallas, Austin, and El Paso vote blue with Fort Worth being the only red city. With low voting turnouts and smaller win margins in the urban centers, Democrats fail to make up what they lose to Republicans in the suburbs, small cities, and rural areas of Texas. Outside the cities, GOP candidates roll up crushing margins of 70 percent or more over Democrats. It is long past time to re-spin the old political saying about a person being born a "D" and dying a "D" in the Lone Star State to reflect the new red reality of taking the first breath and the last in Texas as a Republican.

As was stated in Chapter Four, many Democrats pin their hopes for regaining political control on the future demographic changes showing Hispanic population growth coupled with a numerical decline of Anglos in the state. These trends probably are irreversible but not fatal for Republicans as Hispanic support and voting turnout is not where the D's need them to be to win statewide races. While Hispanics outside of Texas vote nearly 70 percent blue, this has not been so in the Lone Star State where the second largest racial-ethnic group has been much more supportive of the GOP. Looking back at Hispanic support for Republican gubernatorial candidates shows George W. Bush receiving 49 percent in 1998, Rick Perry polling 35-40 percent in his three elections, and Greg Abbott getting 44 percent of the Latino vote in 2014. After the 2012 presidential election, many national Republican strategists suggested that the GOP could not win the White House unless the party showed more support from non-whites. This political calculation is a tricky one for the Texas GOP in light of the fact it wipes out state Democrats with white voters. With its better than national numbers, Texas Republicans seem content to play the white-Anglo party base as long as Hispanics do not go African-American or 90-10 against the party.

The occasional call for Republicans to open up the party to appeal more to minorities in Texas is not new. In 1974 one of the authors (KB) was a delegate to the Republican state convention in Houston. A young Republican and recent graduate of the University of Texas at El Paso (UTEP), KB went before the GOP platform committee to recommend that his party make a greater appeal to blacks and browns in Texas as the Democrats were doing so little for people of color. State Representative Ray Barnhart, the platform committee chairman, reacted to the political science graduate's suggestion with derision and questioned whether or not "the kid" was a true Republican. It may have taken close to 25 years, but Barnhart has been proven right and the author wrong from the game of politics standpoint. It is the GOP that continues to win by appealing to its large Anglo base with no big voter uprising against the R's from the Latino community.

The last reason assuring the future preeminence of Republicans in Texas has to do with the GOP control over the drawing of state legislative lines. Redistricting is a legal requirement for all 50 states after the 10 year U.S. Census is completed. Unless the Democrats can win a majority of state legislative seats in 2020, the Republicans will control the House and the Senate until the 2030s.

The Legislature currently has the reds enjoying a 2-1 membership advantage over the blues which puts the GOP holding all the political redistricting cards.

What redistricting means for political parties in Texas is that the members of the Legislature have the authority to draw new boundary lines for the 150 House and 31 Senate seats. Partisanship is at its highest during a session where line drawing can determine victory or defeat for members and majority party or minority party status for the reds and blues. Many people are aware of the old-fashioned practice of gerrymandering which was an art form where new districts were drawn by members to grab a few marginal districts for one party or the other and to protect incumbents of both parties.

The ancient gerrymandering art form has given away these days to an empirical form of gerrymandering using statistics and modern mapping. Science has now superseded art as Texas Republicans in the majority can "pack" as many Democratic voters into as few districts as possible and "crack" or disperse potential blue voters into a number of neighboring districts to dilute the true strength of the D's. David Daley, author of *RATF**KED*, points out that U.S. Democratic House candidates in 2012 received 1.7 million more total votes than Republicans, but they came up 30 seats short of the GOP.

The Republicans may be the political heavies in Texas, but the Democrats in California have done much the same thing. To maintain power, elites and their legislative agents show little shame when it comes to talking like a democrat and acting like a dictator. While the U.S. Supreme Court has stepped in to rule against parties from undermining democracy through racial gerrymandering, it has not done so for political gerrymandering. The opportunity to rule that extreme cases of political gerrymandering are a violation of the 14th Amendment could have happened in 1986 when Indiana Democrats brought such a claim in *Davis v. Bandemer* against Republican Hoosiers, but the court would not go that far in saying what such a standard might be. This clearly was avoidance by the Supremes in the hope that majority parties in the future would not run up the political score too high for their own players. What the federal judges missed is that Texas Republicans and California Democrats know the difference between legal right and wrong, and life for them is good when democratic principles of equality and fairness do not get in the way of their own political power and government control.

Concluding Remarks

The Republican Party control of Texas government began as a hostile federal takeover during the Reconstruction era. This shotgun marriage would become a happy pairing in 1998 and beyond as Lone Star voters elected GOP candidates to all statewide offices. In 2014 Texas remained red, but a deeper shade, as Tea Party Republicans completed a near clean sweep over establishment conservatives in primary elections before winning over Democrats in November. The party of Bush in Texas now was the party of Cruz. On any number of social, economic, and public policy issues, the state GOP takes positions of extreme conservatism. While economic elites once supported the Democratic Party, the have-mores of personal wealth and institutional position see the Republicans as their best political play in the twenty-first century. Elites like the red party's strong beliefs in cutting individual and corporate taxes, holding down public spending, and rolling back government regulations of business. The continued GOP supremacy in Texas appears to have no end in sight due to a variety of reasons from the state's traditional conservative philosophy to the expected Republican control over the next round of legislative redistricting in 2021.

Works Noted

Holzer, Harold and Norton Garfinkle. 2015. *A Just and Generous Nation*. New York: Basic Books.

Phillips, Kevin. 1969. *The Emerging Republican Majority*. New Rochelle, NY: Arlington House.

Perry, Rick. 2010. *FED UP!*. New York: Little, Brown and CO.

Clinton, Hillary. 1996. *It Takes a Village*. New York: Simon & Schuster.

Green, George Norris. 1984. *The Establishment in Texas Politics*. Norman. OK: University of Oklahoma Press.

Daley, David. 2016. *Rat F**cked*. New York: Liveright Publishing Corporation.

CHAPTER SIX

Business and Labor in Texas

President Calvin Coolidge once said that the business of America was business. Governors George W. Bush, Rick Perry, and Gregg Abbott have confirmed Coolidge's belief through their words and deeds. The three Republican chief executives have made certain that the "bidness" of Texas government is to preserve and protect the interests of commerce and property. No one today doubts that companies and corporations reign supreme in the Lone Star State. The combined efforts of political and economic elites insure that Texas stays near the top of national ratings as one of the most business-friendly states in America with a number two spot behind Utah in a 2016 CNBC ranking.

The business takeover of Texas was not in the original plans of those who designed a new state government in 1875. As was pointed out in Chapter Two, the goal of the Grange was to restrict the taxing and spending powers of government. After the voters approved the proposed constitution, farmers and ranchers felt they would be free from state meddling into their lands, crops, cattle, and lives.

With the evolution of Texas from a rural to an urban state, political control has shifted from landowners to business owners. Although the 1876 Constitution was not written for corporate elites, they would come to appreciate their valuable government inheritance of weak state powers. Political science research has shown that where governments are weak, interest groups will be strong, and in Texas this means business.

It will be our task in this chapter to look at business and labor, and what these interest groups represent for elites and masses. In a perfect world, all interests would carry equal weight in a pluralist system where the checking and balancing of multiple groups would bring about no one dominant group or class. But Texas is far from perfect and worse than most states, as business interests rule with labor historically being the only organized force representing the common man. In his majestic work on *Politics, Parties, and Pressure Groups*, V.O. Key notes that business is the most "potent" interest in the American governmental system. Writing in the 1950s, Key saw the political power of agricultural interests on the wane, and labor's battles with business resulting in just marginal degrees of policy success for workers.

Riding High in Texas

While business power in Washington has fluctuated from Key's day through the 1970s until the present, the political control of Texas business elites has been rock solid over the same 70 years. What Chandler Davidson called the super-rich, or the 99 individuals with a net worth over $50 million, and corporate elites, identified as the 610 directors of top financial institutions headquartered in Texas, kept the Lone Star State a heaven or at least a haven for commerce through the years. The super-rich and institutional directors identified by Davidson in the late 1980s are no longer a part of the current scene. As the scene changes, however, certain prominent families and major institutions continue to insure that elite political goals are met often at mass expense.

A casual look at Davidson's 99 of 30 years ago turns up some familiar Texas names, such as Perry Bass, Dolph Briscoe, Bill Clements, Trammel Crow, Michael Halbouty, Nelson Bunker Hunt, and others. While death has taken away many of the 99, their sons and daughters have stepped in to advance the family's economic interests. It can be expected that when Donald Trump stops dealing, his empire will be taken over by Donald Jr., Ivanka, and Eric.

Despite Mitt Romney's claim that corporations are "people," humans die but corporations are often immortal. To live forever, corporations must continue to achieve economic and political success. To be successful, corporate leaders know that governments play a major role in determining business success. Government taxing, spending, and regulating powers can help or hurt the bottom line, so company executives must be ever vigilant in guiding government hands to do the right thing for them.

How do business interests get government officials to do their bidding? The answer is through active engagement in Washington and Austin through their physical and fiscal presence. In looking at Texas business groups, Cal Jillson divides these groups into two main categories: peak associations and trade associations. The Texas Association of Business, an offshoot of the U.S. Chamber of Commerce, is the chief peak association representing general business interests in the state. Major trade associations in Texas look out for the economic well-being of oil and gas, homebuilding and construction, insurance and banking, hotel and entertainment, and roads and transportation interests. In his first legislative session as a Texas House member, one of the authors (KB) was told by party leaders that "You never mess with oil and gas here if you want to get anything done and to be around for a while."

In addition to peak and trade associations, professional

associations abound in Austin which are dedicated to advancing and protecting the interests of their high income members. Some of these major associations are: the Texas Medical Association, Texas Hospital Association, Texas Bar Association, and the Texas Association of Realtors. It is not uncommon for professional groups to expose their invisible face, as described in Chapter One, by defeating reform proposals that would benefit the people, such as lowering service costs or redefining occupational licensing requirements.

Business Under Attack

At times some individuals will look back longingly to a past era when things appeared to be so much better. For laissez faire capitalists, the wish is to return to the day when business was king over government and labor as industrial giants with the last names of Carnegie, Vanderbilt, and Rockefeller ruled in America. It was a great shock to free enterprisers when President Franklin Roosevelt and Texas Governor James Allred upset their world in the 1930s. Roosevelt and Allred transformed the nation and the state political and economic systems that brought public praise and upper-class condemnation. The business reaction to the New Deal and its support of the working man took one form of counterattack with the passage of the Taft-Hartley Act. This anti-union law restricted national labor rights, and Texas quickly passed a state right-to-work law to further tie the hands of employees in the workplace.

No one should underestimate how important it is to business to have a union free environment. Without unions employers are free to be as good or bad as they choose to be to their employees. In Texas this has meant more bad than good for the masses as the state work history includes the days of slave labor, sharecropping labor, cheap labor, migrant labor, minimum wage labor, undocumented labor, part-time labor, and contract labor with no benefits. The one hope for workers to achieve a good job with good wages and benefits was through unionization. While unions offered a lifeline to workers, economic elites saw unions as a hangman's noose killing off profits. With labor stymied by national and state legislators, business leaders were free to pursue profits without much political opposition until the 1970s.

The social movements of the Watergate decade centered on consumer, environmental, civil, and public interest rights. These rights movements offered a potential threat to the political and economic grip of business leaders in America and Texas. Truth be told, national elites had a great deal more to worry about than state elites where the Lone Star political history of top-down control was a stone unturned during this time of establishment upheaval.

Conservative voices friendly to business began speaking out in the 1970s against what they called a "new class" that threatened democratic capitalism in America. This new class centered in university, media, and public interest circles, and its challenge to business authority was as real as labor's assault during the 1930s and 1940s. The early warning alarms against a new class political takeover and the rise of participatory democracy came from prominent pro-business figures like Michael Novak, Samuel Huntington, and Lewis Powell.

In *The American Vision*, Novak advocated that corporations go on the ideological attack against new class interests by supporting writers, commentators, and researchers who will get out the "business is good for all" message. For Huntington, his directive to economic leaders was to take seriously the excesses of democracy that encouraged increased political participation and government demands. As the author of the U.S. section of *The Crisis of Democracy*, this distinguished Harvard professor believed that too much democracy can be a bad thing for an American political system under great stress in the Nixon years.

It would take a future Supreme Court Justice Lewis Powell to get the X's and O's down for big business in a 1971 confidential memo to the U.S. Chamber of Commerce. Powell believed that corporations were under political attack and must respond forcefully to defeat their enemies. Jacob Hacker and Paul Pierson note that the business counterattack in the 1970s was swift and sweeping: a domestic version of the "Shock and Awe" military doctrine. Hacker and Pierson write in *Winner-Take-All Politics* that corporate Washington public affairs offices went from 100 in 1968 to 500 in 1978, that the number of business firms with registered lobbyists expanded from 175 in 1971 to 2,500 in 1982, and that the number of corporate political action committees grew from 300 in 1976 to 1,200 PACs by the mid-1980s. It was clear that the business community got Powell's message to fight or die, because hostile interests were on the rise in the nation's capital.

While business setbacks in Washington can reverberate in Texas, the state political environment in the 1970s for corporations was battle free compared to the new class challenge to national economic figures. What business had going for it in Texas was a historic hatred of government culture, a one-party political system under elite control, a legal system favoring property over people, and masses living apolitical lives of quiet acceptance of the status quo.

Taxing, Spending, and Regulating

To consider business as a monolithic political force in Texas is an oversimplification as differences exist among the various economic sectors in the state. What all components in the business world have in common is a commitment to increased profits and wealth. Since the 1930s Texas businessmen have not lost sight of the potential threats posed by government agencies and other interest groups to their desire to maintain Texas as a free enterprise state.

How has business accomplished so much in the Lone Star State that makes it the envy of capitalists around the nation? The

Texas heritage that Daniel Elazar identified as a combination of traditionalistic and individualistic subcultures is a good starting point. Elazar saw Texas as a state where business took precedent over government, and economic elites held power and control in a conservative and custodial way over the citizens. For business to be king in Texas, financial leaders realized that they must use the state government powers of taxing, spending, and regulating for their own benefit without arousing any public reaction. The historical record of elites controlling these three state powers is clear with business posting wins and non-business groups ending up with ties and losses.

Taxes it has been said are the price people pay for civilization; it can also be said that the tax bill in Texas rarely ends up in upper-class hands. The Texas tax structure is one of the most regressive in the nation with the burden falling on the masses in the form of sales taxes, property taxes, and user fees. In her 50 state survey of tax laws, Susan Pace Hamill refers to the Lone Star State as one of the "sinful six" states, where the poor pay a much larger share of their income to government than the rich and receive minimal government services in return.

While the Texas tax system benefits the rich over the poor, it also rewards business interests with a free ride, because there is no corporate income tax which is a rarity among the 50 states. When questioned about no corporate income taxes, business representatives are quick to point out that Texas has no personal income tax as if the two were Siamese twins. Having no corporate and individual income taxes works well for elites but poorly for the masses. Wealthy Americans despise federal and state income taxes and will do all they can to avoid paying them. In Texas high rollers only have to worry about Uncle Sam every April 15 and not the state tax man. In response to a Hillary Clinton suggestion during the first 2016 presidential debate that he may have paid no income tax for years, Donald Trump smugly said, "That makes me smart," a sentiment shared by many of the U.S. one-percenters.

Would a state income tax be good for average earners? The short answer is "Yes." This progressive tax generally exempts low-income earners from paying anything and could be a major step in undoing the Texas regressive tax system. Because of Lieutenant Governor Bob Bullock, the chances of a future state income tax are about as good as a person winning the Powerball Jackpot lottery. It was Bullock who made one of the all-time Texas political flip-flops from proposing the idea of an income tax in 1991 to leading the charge for a constitutional amendment passed in 1993 forbidding a future income tax without voter approval. What this means is that another amendment would need to be passed to repeal the 1993 Bullock amendment, an unlikely situation as it would take the "yes" votes of 100 state representatives, 21 senators, and the electorate.

While business has the tax system on its side, the government spending power also has been under corporate control. The rich have kept a tight reign over state expenditures, especially the funding of domestic programs directed to helping people in need. The fear of white, wealthy Texans is that their tax dollars will be raised and spent on minorities. By keeping government spending down means more profits for business and more money staying in private hands.

Cal Jillson, author of *Lone Star Tarnished*, has written that the Texas Way of government taxing and spending limitations is no way to meet future demographic changes and state needs. The Texas conundrum in the coming decades is how the Lone Star State will meet the challenge of the required government service expansion in light of the Republican attachment to private goods and tax cuts. Wealthy Texans want no part of public transportation, public education, public recreation, public neighborhood security, and most other public service systems. For high income individuals, opposing government spending makes good economic sense as they drive their own cars on toll roads, they send their children to private schools and colleges, they participate in sports and activities at private clubs, they pay for private security police in gated communities, and they rely on private physicians and family attorneys to keep them healthy and well-off. There is no question that life in Texas is great for the top dogs and fat cats.

With the strong influence of the wealthy over Texas taxing and spending decisions, government regulation is the third major area of state public power. One of the great American economic myths is that business is anti-regulation. Nothing could be further from the truth; business is pro-government or anti-government regulation depending on how regulation works out for corporate goals or interests. If a free market without government laws and regulations means more profits, then free enterprise it is. When government rules will mean a business windfall or a corporate bailout for a failing company, then it is time for Uncle Sam or Sam Houston to stand up for corporate welfare. For in America, the rich have always favored socialism for themselves and capitalism for the poor. Texas business leaders are most guilty of this hypocrisy over the years as many regulations and laws have been designed to advance private interests often at public expense.

In response to industry pressure, the state of Texas has fought federal environmental laws, especially the push for clean air during the Perry and Abbott years. The suing of the federal government on behalf of "Texas" to preserve unhealthy environmental conditions is held up as public service by many state Republicans who are climate change deniers. In 1969 one of the authors (BL) was stationed in the military at Fort Bliss in El Paso and remembers sergeants telling the troops not to drink the water in Juarez. Army sergeants should be telling the troops in Houston today not to breathe the air. In the twenty-first century, Republicans continue to fight national laws to keep workers safe in the oil fields, in the chemical plants, and at construction sites. The reason for GOP opposition revolves around costs to businesses and the intrusion of the hated Washington nanny state.

When nonbusiness groups from labor, civil rights, and church organizations have come to the defense of employees and workers, their fight has too often been met with state government indifference. For economic elites, doing the wrong thing often is profitable as long as the wrongs do not explode into the public domain. Enron was a great company until it turned out to be a fraud costing investors and employees their financial lives. BP was a great company until the Deepwater Horizon disaster drowned the Gulf Coast in 200 million gallons of oil. Blue Bell was a great company making ice cream to die for until listeria tragically proved the point. In today's winner-take-all business culture, corporate greed is at the center of many company actions putting lives at risk.

The absence of state government regulations is a bonanza for business as Texas is a right-less state. As an employee, a person has no rights against being fired at any time for no stated reason. The renter has few rights but to leave when the property owners say so. Without government zoning laws, the homeowner can only watch, as one of the authors (BL) did, when a used car lot appeared one day across from his Houston Heights house.

As a pro-business state, Texas has rewarded the have-mores and haves with wealth and comfort. The state clearly has been on their side as first Democrats and now Republicans have understood the divine imperative of serving capital in the Capitol. It is as Agriculture Commissioner Jim Hightower once said that Jesus threw the moneychangers out of the temple and they landed in the Texas Legislature.

The relationship between business and labor in the state has been a struggle over the meaning of fair treatment for the past 80 years. Most of the contests of divided wills have gone the employer's way as their superior economic resources and political clout have determined most outcomes. Like a second division sports team, labor continues to compete with business in the hope for a future reversal of fortunes as happened for the Chicago Cubs in 2016.

It was over 100 years ago when a reporter asked Samuel Gompers, the first president of the American Federation of Labor (AFL), what labor wanted? Gompers' one word answer was, "More."

His answer highlights the economic side of the union movement which has never been lost on Texas business leaders. With just over 500,000 union members in 2015, Texas ranks among the bottom five states in terms of the percentage of unionized employees. New York City alone has 900,000 unionists who will see their state minimum wage raised to $15 per hour by 2018. In Houston the 2017 wage rate is at the federal minimum of $7.25. It is the unshakeable belief of Texas elites that more money for the masses means less money for them.

No Department of Labor

While traveling in Arkansas, one of the authors (RS) noticed a highway sign pointing to an exit for the state Department of Labor office. The fact that Arkansas which gave America Walmart, one of the most anti-union companies around, has a government agency looking out for workers' rights is a surprise. The fact that Texas has no Department of Labor guaranteeing employee rights related to pay, a safe and healthy work environment, and anti-discrimination job protection is no surprise.

The closest the Lone Star State comes to a Labor Department is the Texas Workforce Commission (TWC). In the *Texas State Directory*, this commission is listed on the last page of all state agencies, boards, and commissions. Fairness might say that this listing is due to alphabetical ordering, but the authors are not completely convinced. Among its tasks, the TWC provides workforce development, offers industry information and analysis, and administers the state unemployment compensation program. With three gubernatorial appointed commissioners, this agency has no Norma Raes on board and is no advocate for Texas employees.

If the Texas Workforce Commission is no labor advocate, the state does have a Department of Insurance (TDI) governing workers' compensation. The TDI has no Occupational Safety and Health

Authority (OSHA) like powers to provide for safe workplaces or to investigate on-the-job complaints. It can be noted that Texas remains the only state that does not require employers to carry workers' compensation insurance for those injured on the job.

While state agencies do little to watch out for the well-being of workers, Texas does have labor unions. Texas labor today is made up of three worker categories: unionized private sector employees, unionized public sector employees, and nonunionized employees. From a worker's perspective, the best category for the employed is to be a private unionist where wages, hours, and benefits are covered under a collective bargaining agreement between labor and management. The authority of the National Labor Relations Board exists as a referee between the two sides should its intervention become necessary. The practical effect for the workers in private sector unions is that they receive higher pay, better health care and retirement benefits, greater job security and legal protection, and more respect from employers through the force of a union contract than the boss's handshake given to nonunion workers. In 2015 some of the biggest Texas private sector unions were the Communications Workers of America (CWA), the United Steelworkers (USW), the International Brotherhood of Electrical Workers (IBEW), and the United Auto Workers (UAW).

Without collective bargaining agreements and no legal right to strike, public union employees, the second worker category, have their hands tied compared to their private sector brothers and sisters. The largest public sector unions affiliated with the AFL-CIO in the Lone Star State are the American Federation of Teachers (AFT), the American Federation of Government Employees (AFGE), and the International Association of Fire Fighters (IAFF). While Texas government unionists have tied hands, they still are better off than nonunionized employees stuck at work with no contract, no voice, and no rights. What state and local government unions can do is to use the power of their mass numbers to work on behalf of members. Police, fire, and teacher union leaders in major Texas cities have been successful in "meeting and discussing" economic and noneconomic issues with local government officials. Union success or failure often stems from the amount of political power labor can exercise along with its ability to marshal general public support to its side.

With no contract and no political power, the true proletarians in the Texas work force today are nonunionized employees. These workers go to the office, store, plant, or factory each day not knowing that this could be their last day of employment in "at will" Texas. In right-to-work states, employers hold all the cards, and workers can be fired at any time without prior notice and reason given for termination. To avoid a shocked fired worker "going postal," bosses have learned the art of using human resources personnel and private security guards to insure a speedy and clean exit from the workplace.

In *Hispanics in the Workplace*, anti-union attorney Jacob Monty advises managers to explain to their Hispanics employees that they are no longer working in a foreign country but are working in Texas, where no one is entitled to notice of a job loss or front pay. Front pay or "Indemnification" is provided to terminated workers in some Latin American countries, but the door and not dollars is what let-go employees receive in the Lone Star State. To avoid any misunderstanding, Monty suggests that companies have their Latino employees sign a statement acknowledging their at-will status before starting any job.

Politics and Unions

Lacking the deep financial pockets of business, labor's political game is more visible than invisible as it seldom has a seat at the state or local government table. Through electoral politics, private and public sector unions affiliated with the national and state AFL-CIO try to make a difference for their members and workers in general. Labor screens candidates, makes political endorsements, works to elect its "friends," and to defeat its "foes." Candidates running for local offices in heavily populated metropolitan areas aggressively seek out the AFL-CIO election endorsement in non-partisan races. In partisan contests, the D's and R's following candidate names on the ballot may be at cross purposes with labor's choices. Many Democrats and union members may not have followed the Harris County Central Labor Council's endorsement of Republican Ed Emmett over Democrat Gordon Quan in the 2010 county judge's election won by labor-supported Emmett. For elections without party labels, Republican voters especially are more apt to consider following the endorsements of police, fire, and teacher unions in casting their votes.

The union political involvement in electoral politics can range from official endorsements, to cash contributions, to phone bank operations, and to get-out-the-vote efforts targeting jobsites and selected neighborhoods. Labor's boots-on-the-ground operations are unparalleled among Texas interest groups. In low turnout elections, unions can magnify their political clout by their superior turnout capacity. As measured by the Harris County AFL-CIO Council, labor turns out its voters more than two-and-one-half times the average of the general population in its endorsed races. The sophistication of unions in pinpointing members and other potential voting supporters has grown exponentially in the era of metrics-driven electioneering. One big plus for labor in elections is its ability to inform, to educate, and to activate its membership all within the legal parameters of federal law. This makes business interests envious as they often have to rely on their political action committees and paid help to do the same thing.

The 2015 Houston city election showed labor's political strength in a mayoral race won by state Representative Sylvester Turner on his third office try. The Harris County Central Labor Council and unions representing police, fire, and teachers were early supporters of the second African-American ever elected to the top city post. Turner's runoff election victory margin over his business-backed opponent Bill King was just 4,086 votes out of 212,696. With just 200,000 plus runoff votes cast in a city of 2.1 million people, labor's strength was magnified along with its traditional allies in the Democratic Party and the black, brown, and gay communities as a miniscule number of citizens showed up at the polls on December 12. The Turner 2015 victory also marked the first time that the AFL-CIO used the U. S. Supreme Court's Citizens United ruling decision to establish an independent expenditure group, Worker's Voice, to spend union funds to contact and convince nonunion voters to back labor's candidates.

Pocket Book or Prayer Book?

No matter the person or the group, it is almost un-American not to agree with Gompers' "more" sentiment in a U.S. consumer, capitalist society. "Show me the money" is the Texas state anthem as business and labor groups race for the green. Like business, labor is not a monolith as some unions vary in their commitments to economic and noneconomic goals. Depending on the union, members will differ in their political outlooks, and what they expect in return for their union dues. For private sector unions, the main focus may be on the financial package in the labor-management negotiated contract. For public sector unions, the chief concern may be on the legal standing and job security of members.

In either case these differences can translate into some members carrying the union slate card into a polling place, while other members throw away the card as soon as it is handed to them. Like the general public, union members do not always vote in their own economic interests and may be unaware of just what these interests are. Texas elites have always been good at "helping" the masses to embrace their definition of what would be best for them. One can always be assured that rich people think they know what is best for themselves and others time and again.

With so many Texas elections focusing on God, guns, and gays, unions have had to walk a narrow line in order not to lose their members to the noneconomic three G's. It has been especially tough for unions with progressive economic goals to stay clear of the gun issue as many union members are NRA supporters and Second Amendment zealots. What Texas labor has tried to do is to wave the pocketbook and not the prayer book before its members with a sprinkling of support for public education, infrastructure improvement, and equal justice for all.

While most of labor's political backing has gone to Democrats in partisan elections, this is no guarantee of policy goal success. If ever there were time to repeal the state's anti-union right-to-work law, it was in the early 1990s when liberal Democrat Ann Richards was governor and numerous progressive D's were in office. Richards and the other blues waved the white flag of surrender without any political effort to free Texas labor from the right-to-work-for-less provision of Texas law. As was pointed out in Chapters Four and Five, state Republicans have never hidden their opposition to organized labor, but Democrats have been the party of hypocrisy as they have pretended to be for workers and the people in words but not in their Austin deeds.

One of the authors (RS) learned this lesson all too well in 1999 when as secretary treasurer of the Harris County AFL-CIO Council he called on former Lieutenant Governor Bill Hobby over what he thought to be a minor oversight. His call to the Senate leader was to remind him about the construction situation surrounding the building of the new Hobby Center in downtown Houston. The standard practice among many builders on private projects was to use cheap labor provided by nonunion and undocumented workers.

Thinking this was no big deal, RS reminded Bill Hobby about Houston's prevailing wage standard on government contracts, which is the U.S. Department of Labor's hourly pay scales on public construction projects, and how some contractors were underpaying skilled labor on the city project. Always union-endorsed in every election, this long time Democratic official expressed outrage when told of the situation and the request to make things right. Hobby accused the author of trying to "extort" public funds by getting a high-placed "friend" to support a city rule that would only have meant more money for construction workers.

Houston Gets Hope

Texas labor unions have had few victories in the twenty-first century as Republicans in power are opposed to most of their goals. Because state law prohibits collective bargaining rights for government employees, union growth has been slow and difficult. Texas law does allow, however, local voters in home rule cities to approve public employee collective bargaining. Voters in San Antonio and El Paso have done so for police and firefighter unions.

Absent bargaining, unions can engage in another practice known as "meet and confer," which is a watered-down version of collective bargaining. Meet and confer status comes about only if the Legislature authorizes this practice for a specific city, and local government officials give their approval as Houston, Austin, and Fort Worth have done for police and fire unions.

Because conservative Democrats and Republicans see no public relations or political value in backing bargaining rights, civilian city employees have been without these rights. It has been good election politics for conservative D's and R's to have the campaign endorsements of first responders who put their lives on the line for local residents. Other government employees, such as garbage workers, clerks, secretaries, and road crews, often are minority group members who do not offer the same political value to elected officials as do cops and firefighters.

In 2007 two unions, the American Federation of State, City and Municipal Employees (AFSCME) and the State Employees International Union (SEIU), sought to get the Legislature to approve "meet and confer" status for the 13,000 non-uninformed Houston workers. This task was monumental as Republicans held over 80 House seats and 19 Senate seats, and it was no secret that the GOP's disdain for unions stems from their economic and political beliefs.

For AFSME and SEIU to get a legislative win would require some Austin magic. Using their access to Republican Speaker Tom Craddick, the Craddick Democrats got the speaker to go along with the unions' plan. One of the authors (KB) was the House bill sponsor, who got the Houston "Meet" bill through his Urban Affairs Committee by a 6-0 vote. In the Senate, Republican Lieutenant Governor David Dewhurst had supported such meeting measures in the past for police and fire unions. It was Democratic Senator John Whitmire, a Dewhurst ally and friend, who managed the measure for Houston's non-uniformed employees through the upper house. It was a stroke of luck for unions that two Democrats had Republicans in high places willing to let "meet and confer" go forward for floor votes.

Passing in the House 98-37 and in the Senate 31-0, the Houston bill went on to Republican Rick Perry for his signature. The governor signed the bill into law with a provision that would allow voters to override any future city government negotiated contract with public civilian employees. This Texas labor legislative victory was one of the biggest wins for unions in the South in the twenty-first century. It opened the door for the creation of the Houston Organization of Public Employees (HOPE), a 13,000 municipal workers union. HOPE is one of the largest unions in the Lone Star State with Houston becoming one of the few Southern cities allowing bargaining rights over wages, hours, and working conditions for government employees not fighting crimes or fires.

The magician's trick of getting HOPE for Houston relied on political alliances, sleight-of-hand skills, and public darkness. Having two well-connected Democrats working with Republican legislative leaders was a major factor in the big labor win. The other factors contributing to a union victory came from the sponsors' acceptance of an optional public vote to permit bargaining and their willingness to maintain silence about the labor bill. Although the bill applied to Houston only, KB and Whitmire still kept the measure on the down low in order to keep it away from right wing blogs. Had the anti-union forces understood what was going on and raised strong objections, Republicans would have killed the bill.

Business, Labor, and Education

Betting on business to win in Texas and labor to lose will make gamblers money over the long haul. Union victories in the state generally are more about killing bad legislation than accomplishing policy wins for workers. There have been times when business and labor have been on the same side in Austin as occurred during the era of Governor Mark White in the 1980s. It was a coming together of traditional rivals on education that brought a win-win situation for all as real gains were made in education funding, classroom standards, teacher pay, and educational employee rights.

Business and labor supported important pieces of legislation that improved public schools for students from all backgrounds. To get these gains, labor accepted the business demand that all teachers be retested to determine their classroom competency. This was seen by many teachers as a professional insult as they were college graduates and already certified Texas teachers. To keep their certificates, teachers had to pass a reading, writing, and math test. In many cases this was a tough price to pay as it resulted in the voluntary and involuntary departure of some teachers from their chosen profession.

Following the White era of support for education reform, business interests began to retreat from education and to stick to its main concern over profits and losses. With Republican ascendency and control over state government, economic elites began their opposition to public education in the form of massive spending cuts, the promotion of non-public school choice, vouchers, charter school funding, attacks on teacher organizations, and requirements for excessive student testing.

In the Houston Independent School District, inner-city schools began losing enrollment to charter schools. Fewer students meant budget cuts resulting in reducing the number of support positions, such as nurses, librarians, and counsellors. Without these support service personnel, some schools fell in performance and enrollment causing harm to students and the closing of doors in some cases.

The Texas business-labor divide on public education has deepened over the past years, and the fissures can be seen at the local and state government levels. In the electoral politics of school boards, labor's endorsed candidates for the Houston school district were not the same as the business community's candidates. Both at the local and state level, officials supporting education budget cuts had business backing. As school funding was reduced and more money went to charters, an economy-of- scale effect ensued. Neighborhood schools with low enrollments simply could not offer what these schools needed to provide. While such schools received their "equal" education dollar allocation, many needed more funds to adequately educate their students. This issue of adequate school funding for students especially living in poor neighborhoods has now become a legal and legislative matter for state courts and the Texas House and Senate to resolve.

While business took a long nap from public education matters, it recently has taken a keen interest in education. The business wakeup call is due to its inability to find trained workers for so-called middle-skill jobs within the Texas labor force. As the workforce has aged and retired, there are skilled labor shortages in manufacturing, construction, and healthcare. During the 1990s, public schools largely abandoned their vocational programs, now called Career and Technical Education (CTE), to prepare students to go to college.

In the Houston area, the Greater Houston Partnership (formerly known as the Houston Chamber of Commerce) has an entire initiative built around middle-skill job training and has been lobbying hard for public school education interventions to create a pipeline of workers for middle jobs. What has been seen is the usual business hand wringing about future workforce needs. It will be interesting to see if any of this actually translates into business support in 2017 and beyond for education funding increases to meet the state CTE and other educational needs with a Legislature used to abdicating its responsibilities to students.

One of the authors (RS) remembers a meeting with the Houston business community on the subject of educating for the future based on labor projections. At the meeting, the discussion turned to skilled work shortages in Texas, and one prominent businessman said that wages, benefits, and training would have to be increased to get the needed skilled workers. Along with these necessary increases, the leader said that comprehensive immigration reform would also be a requirement. The looks around the room said everything as the audience members bowed their heads to avoid eye contact with the speaker and the one labor leader (RS) present. Economics aside, the political question is will the business-backed governor, lieutenant governor, and Republican legislators, who cut educational funding in the past, do an about-face on the issue for what the state economy requires in the future?

Concluding Remarks

This chapter began by looking at business which has been riding high during urbanized Texas times. Business elites representing general and specific interests hold a tight grip over government. While national elites had to worry over a new class challenge, state elites were more focused on maintaining the Texas high pro-business rating. This rating has come about by the strong corporate influence over Austin's taxing, spending, and regulatory powers.

While business represents well the state haves, labor has been the one political voice for the have-nots. With a Texas culture and government working against organized labor, unions continue to represent and fight on behalf of their private and public sector members. While business has wealth as its greatest resource, labor has had to rely on its general base of supporters and political campaign clout to achieve some wins. At times labor's Democratic allies have worked with Republicans to bring HOPE to Houston and education reform to Texas.

Works Noted

Key V.O. Jr. 1958. *Politics, Parties, and Pressure Groups.* New York: Thomas Y. Crowell.

Davidson, Chandler. 1990. *Race and Class in Texas Politics.* Princeton, NJ: Princeton University Press.

Elazar, Daniel J. 1972. *American Federalism.* New York: Thomas Y. Crowell

Jillson, Cal. 2011. *Texas Politics* New York: Routledge.

Novak, Michael. 1978. *The American Vision.* Washington, D.C.: American Enterprise Institute.

Crozier, Michael and Samuel P. Huntington. 1975. *The Crisis of Democracy.* New York: New University Press.

Hacker, Jacob S. and Paul Pierson. 2010. *Winner-Take-All Politics.* New York: Simon & Schuster.

Hamill, Susan Pace. 2007. *As Certain as Death.* Durham, NC: Carolina Academic Press.

Jillson, Cal. 2015. *Lone Star Tarnished.* New York: Routledge.

Monty, Jacob M. 2011. *Hispanic's in the Workplace.* Houston: Emporion Press.

Texas State Directory 2016, Austin: Texas State Directory Press.

CHAPTER SEVEN

LEGISLATURES IN TEXAS

On April Fool's Day in 1979, Bo Byers, the Austin bureau chief for the *Houston Chronicle*, wrote an opinion editorial piece entitled "The Flood of Special Interest Bills" for his newspaper. Decrying how much special interest legislation members were pushing, Byers said that the 66th Texas Legislature might go down in the political history books as "The Special Interest Texas Legislature." The Byers article should be required reading for all Texans as every legislative session since then has been a meeting where private interests prevailed over public concerns.

It is a sad Lone Star State of affairs when the Legislature, thought of by political theorists as the people's branch of government, has so thoroughly fallen into the pockets of the privileged as the general interest needs largely go unattended. This may be the way of the Texas world today, but the constitutional authors of Article III had not intended the Senate and House to operate as institutions dedicated to helping the haves at the expense of the have-nots.

In many respects, the Texas Legislature is the most powerful government branch within a formal system of three weak political institutions. For it is the Legislature, and not the executive or the judiciary, that has the responsibility of carrying out the four major state functions of making the laws, establishing a budget, overseeing administrative agencies, and representing the people in government. Of the four state functions, establishing a budget is the only constitutional requirement imposed on the Legislature in a regular session. During the 85th session, legislators passed a state budget of $217 billion for 2018 and 2019.

What the Framers Wrought

Just like the national government framers, the Texas framers intended the Legislature to be the leading branch as it was listed first in the 1876 Constitution ahead of the executive and the judiciary. This first was intended, however, to be a "weak" first as Chapter Two pointed out in that the constitutional authors favored very limited government. From the nineteenth to the twenty-first century, the limits have shone through in a number of structural and functional areas. Like all other states but Nebraska, the Texas Legislature is a bicameral body consisting of a Senate and a House of Representatives. Article III set the number of members at 31 senators and 93 representatives with a provision allowing the House to expand to 150 depending on future population growth. When the state population hit 1.7 million in 1881, the House expanded in size to the constitutional maximum of 150.

With its 181 state legislators, Texas most closely resembles Vermont with its 30 senators and 150 representatives. Being just like Bernie Sanders' home state might be enough to cause Republicans in Austin to think about expanding the size of the Legislature. Among all 50 states, the Senate numerical high is Minnesota at 67 with the low being Alaska at 20; the respective House high and low numbers are New Hampshire at 400 and Alaska at 40. The Lone Star State's numbers are not out of line with other large states:

California (120), Florida (160), and New York (218). Texas citizens might be helped if the number of legislative districts was increased as more members from smaller electoral units could enhance the ability of the people to fight back against the special interest lock over the Legislature. It has been the history of elites to favor fewer people voting in a political system and to keep the number of elected officials to a minimum so as to maximize their control over government. While size always matters in a democracy, the biennial nature of regular legislative sessions has come to be valued and defended by the powers that be. Texas is only one of four states that has its regular session meeting once every two years. Montana, Nevada, and North Dakota are the other annual meeting skippers, as Arkansas in 2008 and Oregon in 2010 deserted the ranks of the biennials. From a good government basis, annual sessions are an essential, but who wants good government in Texas? Not elites! The upper dogs want a profitable political system for themselves, while the underdogs have been led to believe that good government in Texas is an oxymoron.

34 Steps and 62 Days

All Texas government books have a diagram outlining the steps of how a bill becomes a law. These graphic presentations vary from book to book numbering from as few as 13 steps shown to as many as 34 steps. There is no single book chronicling the history of a Texas law as Stephen Bailey did for the U.S. Employment Act of 1946 in *Congress Makes a Law*. No state book is needed, however, to realize the truth of Senator John Kennedy's comment about his surprise when any bills became law given the number of steps involved in the legislative process.

Most congressional experts generalize and say that the percentage of bills becoming federal law is around three to five percent. Peverill Squire and Gary Moncrief, authors of *State Legislatures*

Today, put the average for all states in 2011 at 18 percent. The Texas figure for the 85th Legislature of 2017 was around a 20 percent passage rate out of 6,631 bills introduced. It may be fun to play with the numbers, but numbers can deceive as Hillary Clinton and the world found out in 2016. The important point to remember about the Texas Legislature is that it meets for 140 days in a 730 day period. The 140 day time frame is misleading as there are just 62 meaningful days to address state needs in every two-year cycle. The official 140 day period hardly gives senators and representatives any time to deliberate in a thoughtful way on important state issues. The 140 days become in reality 62 when constitutional restrictions and House rules are factored into the lawmaking process.

Under the Legislature's procedures, the first 30 days of a regular session is the time for members to introduce bills. The dance of legislation does begin before this time on the first Monday after the November election as state lawmakers can start filing bills. When the session officially commences on the second Tuesday in January of odd-numbered years, the first 30-day bill introduction time means just that as no bill can be considered in committee or on the floor unless the governor has declared it an emergency. As the 2017 regular session was about to begin, Governor Greg Abbott designated four legislative measures as emergency items for immediate consideration. The Abbott emergency measures were directed to fix a broken Child Protective Service Agency, to ban sanctuary cities in Texas, to reform state ethics laws, and to support a states' call for a U.S. constitutional convention to curtail federal government powers.

Following the 30 days of bill introductions, the second 30 days of a session is when standing committees can meet in the Senate and the House to consider assigned bills from the lieutenant governor and the speaker. George Goodwin has called standing committees, *The Little Legislatures,* as they are a vital part of the lawmaking process. Senate and House standing committees are the permanent workhouse committees with around 20 in the upper chamber and 40 in the lower. These significant legislative bodies cover important policy areas, such as public education, criminal justice, natural resources, business and commerce, transportation, insurance, agriculture, and state expenditures and taxation.

During the 30 days of bill introduction and 30 days of committee work, there is no floor activity taking place in the Senate and the House. When the green light for legislation goes on during Day 61 of a session, both supporters and opponents of bills will have the opportunity to discuss, debate, amend, approve, and reject floor measures. The rules of the House of Representatives can throw a wrench in the legislative works as all bills under consideration must be voted on no later than Day 122 of the 140 day session. The House rule effectively meant that in 2017 the time frame for bill making in Texas ran from Day 61, March 11, until Day 122, May 12, or 62 days. This two-month time frame puts Texas government in a tangled mess of having to do two years of serious work in less than half the time of a college semester.

The compression of legislative time is extremely beneficial to the state establishment whose primary goal is to maintain the status quo. For the citizens in need of government action, the refrain of a Houston Texan fan of "wait until next season" can be adjusted to say "wait for two more years" for change, but positive government change for the people seldom occurs. The state legislative process clearly benefits elites and not the masses. The likelihood of passing major public reforms during a two-month period once every two years is a long shot, especially as a lifeblood matter like the two-year state budget has to be addressed. It was understandable in 1991 when Governor Ann Richards took office that she convinced Senate and House leaders to postpone any state budget action during the regular session, and to wait on her call for a special summer session for budget making. Governor Richards knew it would take more than 140 days to pass her legislative goals of insurance reform, a Texas lottery amendment, state agency changes, and to finalize the budget in a regular session.

Who Can Serve and Afford It?

For a job citizens hold in low regard, there are still many prospective candidates seeking Texas Senate and House offices, and no great incumbent exodus from office. In their legislative book, Squire and Moncrief note the 2014 results from a 14-state study that showed Tennessee lawmakers with the highest public approval rating of 49 percent and Washington state legislators with the lowest at 18 percent. During this time frame, Texas members had a 30 percent approval rating.

If a person desires to become a Texas senator or representative, five constitutional or formal requirements must be met. Three are the same for both offices as potential legislators must be United States citizens, qualified Texas voters, and have one-year residency in the district sought prior to Election Day. Two different legal standards for the Senate and the House cover state residency and age. Potential senators must have lived in Texas at least five years prior to election and be at least 26 years old, while future representatives must be two-year residents and 21.

Like most Texas governors, Austin legislators over the years overwhelmingly have been white, male, and Anglo. Today they are Republicans, but throughout most of state history legislators had been Democrats. The main occupational background of the members has gone from farming in the nineteenth century to law in the twentieth to business in the twenty-first. Due to demographic changes and successful Republican gerrymandering, the disappearance of the Anglo Democrat has become a fact of political life. In the 85th Legislature, Democrats held over 60 seats with just seven Anglos sitting on the D side of the aisle. The vanishing white Democrat is unlikely to reappear as Hispanics and African-Americans have taken their places in Austin.

For elected members at all government levels, their salaries are a pittance compared to private sector money. President Donald Trump, a billionaire, decided to wave his measly $400,000 presidential salary. To Trump, $400,000, which is 20 percent below what a first-year major league baseball player makes, is pocket change. To many state legislators around the country, however, their salary is the primary income source.

State legislative pay varies greatly from a high in California of over $95,000 to a low of $0 in New Mexico. The national average for legislators is around $20,000. In Texas senators and representatives make $7,200 per year in salary. Under the 1876 Constitution, a member's salary was set at $460 in the state charter, so that only the voters approving a proposed amendment could raise the amount which was done in 1975 to the current pay level.

How do people serve in the Legislature on a $7,200 salary? With low pay a fact of life from the inaugural session, the job of state legislator was intended as a part-time post. Today's pay level would indicate a continuation of that intention, but the reality for most senators and representatives is that their elected offices are full-time positions. Low pay certainly limits who can run and serve, and this pay level has resulted in the average legislator serving eight years or less. Because they lack an independent income, many people interested in running for a legislative seat are priced out of the position. This situation benefits special interest groups as many legislators become dependent upon the outside employment from these interests, which gives these groups a cozy relationship with state decision makers.

In looking at the Legislature, five types of people have made their way to the Senate and the House. First, wealthy individuals find it easy to be a member. Well-off people have made their money and can devote their time to politics. Wealthy rancher Delwin Jones from Lubbock spent 31 years in Austin, first as a Democrat and then as a Republican. Jones once described his time in the Legislature as "just a hobby."

A second type of server is a member like Representative Charlie Geren, a Republican from Fort Worth, and the owner of the successful Railhead Smokehouse restaurant. Geren represents the member type whose income comes from a business ownership or an affiliation with a law firm back home. During his time in state office, Democratic Representative Sylvester Turner, elected Houston mayor in 2015, was a principal partner in the law firm of Barnes and Turner.

Some legislators are able to serve as they take jobs offered by major private groups wanting access to a friend in a high place. Utility companies like TXU and CenterPoint, insurance companies like State Farm and Allstate, and public tax collectors such as Heard Goggin, have hired this third type of state legislator knowing they can sleep better at night with one of their own embedded in the Senate or the House.

Direct conflicts of interest or honest graft have marked a fourth member type serving in the Legislature. Some members have taken money from lobby groups and gone on to represent these interests in Austin. Republican Representative Gary Elkins of Houston is a payday loan chain owner and a strong opponent of government efforts to regulate the industry. Republican Senator John Carona for years represented firms working for homeowner associations, and he blocked every attempt to limit the power of associations from foreclosing on people's homes for failure to pay minor assessments.

Surprisingly, some members representing a fifth category got elected and never realized the low pay and time requirements of the office. One member, an attorney, had no partners and lost all his clients due to the many special 30 day sessions called that disrupted his legal work. He eventually went bankrupt and had to leave office. Another member's service resulted in personal hard times, as he had to sell his house, live off the equity, and move in with his in-laws to stay financially afloat.

Another money problem related to legislative service is the cost of running a political campaign that has exploded over the past two decades. Candidates spend big money for the few open and competitive contests, but average campaign expenditures are not small change operations. During the 1990s, a person could run a campaign for $50,000 or less. In recent years, the costs have skyrocketed as economic elites have poured money into primary and general election races to insure that their apparatchiks are in the Senate and House. Competitive House campaigns average $250,000 to $400,000 today with some races approaching a million dollars. Senate contests routinely cost a million or more with no ceiling too high. What big rollers get for their campaign contributions are not "bought state senators and representatives," but "rented" ones for the times when a key interest vote comes up.

Types of Legislators

James David Barber and Mark Green have looked at the Connecticut Legislature and the U.S. Congress and classified members in their books on work styles and modes of behavior. While Barber identifies four legislator types from "spectator" to "lawmaker" in *The Lawmakers*, Green has pointed out 10 congressional types from "overachievers" to "absentees and attenders" in *Who Runs Congress?*. Based on these books and the authors' observations, Texas legislators will be divided into eight types from "organization man" to "delegate."

The "organization man," the first type, is an institutionalist committed to the Senate and the House leadership and the parliamentary rules. Often a good soldier and loyal ally, Representatives Pete Gallegos and Craig Washington played these roles well for Speakers Pete Laney and Billy Clayton. The closeness of Gallegos to Speaker Laney in the House caused some members to comment that "there goes Pete and rePete" as the two walked by. Urban liberal Washington bonded with rural conservative Speaker Clayton to constitute a formidable team during their office time together. Two experts on legislative rules and procedures were former Representatives Republican Warren Chisum and Democrat Ron Wilson. The two were masters of points of order which sent many sponsors' bills to their graves.

The Texas Legislature has had many a great "orator," the second legislative type. The orator makes spellbinding floor speeches, gets senators and representatives to sit down and listen in awe, and inspires others to rise above personal politics. Senator Barbara Jordan, the first African-American elected to the upper house in 1966 since Reconstruction, had a voice and delivery worthy of James Earl Jones. During his time in the House, Representative Sylvester Turner's words would stop members in their tracks to think deeply about what he was calling on them to do.

Type three is the "climber" or the member who burns with political ambition. The climber is looking to parlay a current position into something higher on the government ladder. Before he had finished his first House term in 1991, Representative Mike Martin already was planning for a 1992 Senate race and checking out his new office digs, only to lose the race resulting in him being forced out of his old office. Success would come, however, for climbers Senator Dan Patrick with his 2014 lieutenant governor's win and for Representative Joaquin Castro in his 2012 U.S. House victory.

It may surprise the average citizen that some legislators go off to Austin to be "spectators," the fourth legislative type, and not players. For over 30 years, Representative Charles Finnell enjoyed the House view with his biggest career accomplishment being the passage of a law creating a 1-800 number for Texans to call if they saw a railroad arm malfunctioning. After every session, *Texas Monthly* magazine lists four-to-six members as "furniture," meaning that the legislator's performance was "indistinguishable from that of their desks and chairs." In recent sessions, this dishonor has gone to Senator Bob Hall of Edgewood and Representative Hubert Vo of Houston. It may be because he once told a reporter that a trained monkey could do a legislator's job, but Representative Randy Pennington became the ultimate spectator when he waited until May to show up for the 1991 regular session.

While Finnell was content to watch and not learn and Pennington was content not to watch, some Senate and House spectators enjoyed their Austin lives as passive legislators but as active party animals. Before the "Hammer" found Jesus, Representative Tom Delay, sporting a porn star mustache, was known around the Capitol in the 1980s as "Hot Tub Tom." Delay shared a rental property with other good-time members that was known as Macho Manor where wine, women, and song were the house order of the day.

The "advertiser," the fifth legislative type, is an individual on a personal mission. This member type solicits business, makes connections with prominent people, and builds contacts with lobbyists. Senator Boris Miles of Houston has found the legislative life to be good for his insurance and bond business. As a land developer and construction company owner, Representative Cecil Bell of Magnolia has never seen a MUD, or municipal utility district, he did not love. Bell is the MUD champion in Austin as his companies have reaped millions in business contracts from so-called water districts in Texas. Fair or foul, advertisers often come under press and ethical scrutiny over the question of private gain coming from public service.

Making speeches, introducing lots of bills, sending out memos and reports, and always seeming to be in the thick of legislative action is where the "lawmaker," the sixth type, can be found. When he was in the House, Dallas Representative Steve Wolen's colleagues regarded him as the smartest and most effective legislator. Today, the lawmaker label fits Senator John Whitmire of Houston whose impact on the Texas criminal justice system has been greater than any other elected official in Austin.

While the lawmaker is at the center of the legislative ring, the "lone ranger," the seventh type, is an outsider and solitary man. For some lone rangers, their peripheral status comes from a focus on a single issue in which there will be no compromise. During his time in the House, Representative Charlie Hartland of Houston was a moral zealot with his only interests being in stopping abortions in Texas and addressing perverse behavior from an Old Testament standpoint. For Representative Lon Burnam of Fort Worth, his loneliness stemmed from his fight for issues that had no chance of passage and sometimes drew no other vote than his own when the roll was called. Burnam's intransigence drew scorn from other members and a House nickname of Lon "Crash and Burnam."

Congressional scholars, like Roger Davidson, have suggested that there are two main membership roles, the delegate and the trustee, to play within a legislative body. If the lawmaker is looking out for the concerns of the entire community, then the delegate has his eye focused on district or local constituency interests. While Senator Whitmire looked out for state interests in the legal area, a "delegate" legislator turns his attention not to the big policy picture but to matters affecting the daily lives of the home folks. This eighth and final legislative type is represented by the late Senator Mario Gallegos of Houston. As a representative and then a senator, Gallegos worked to help his constituents by fighting for water and sewer lines for his district, by wanting more police patrolling, by backing the removal of wall graffiti, and by moving for a cleanup of salvage yards. These urban refurbishing efforts made sense for the legislator and his city constituency. For Galveston Senator Babe Schwartz and his constituents, the senator's work on government cleanup efforts was aimed at beaches and the coastal regions. It was through the legislative effort of Schwartz that Texas laws were passed covering public access to beach areas and coastal restoration projects.

Leadership Power and Membership Challenges

The lieutenant governor in the Senate and the speaker in the House, the bicameral legislative leaders, wield enormous power in their chambers. Each leader determines members' committee assignments, establishes legislative priorities, and influences what bills will or will not be considered. While most states give the governor the authority to develop and to recommend a budget, this is not the case in Texas. It is the responsibility of the Legislative Budget Board, co-chaired by the lieutenant governor and speaker, to develop budgetary recommendations for state government spending.

The paths to Texas legislative leadership differ greatly from the U.S. Congress where the Republican majority party members elected Senator Mitch McConnell and Representative Paul Ryan to lead the national legislature for 2017-2018. In Texas the Senate leader is the lieutenant governor, chosen by the voters, as was the case of Dan Patrick in 2014. House members do elect the speaker from within their own ranks, but the vote can be bipartisan in nature as happened in 2009 when Republican Joe Straus defeated fellow Republican Tom Craddick, the incumbent speaker, with the help of Democratic members' votes.

In looking at the Senate and House leadership positions over time, it can be said that the post occupants have had a great impact over the lives of all Texans. Considered the single most powerful governmental office, the lieutenant governor is no American vice-president. Lieutenant Governor Bill Hobby, whose father served as both governor and LG, holds the record of 18 years of service from 1973 to 1991 in the Senate top spot. Writing in *How Things Really Work*, Hobby states that in 1959 he knew the post of lieutenant governor was his dream job. The dream would be realized in 1972 when Bill Hobby ran against no incumbent as the dark cloud of a bank scandal discouraged old Austin political faces from running for office. It was the new face of Hobby who won the Democratic primary and had no Republican opponent in the general election. Despite the efforts by fellow Democrats to encourage him to run for governor, the man considered to have been the greatest Texas lieutenant governor ever would not budge. What Bill Hobby understood is that becoming governor probably was a step down for the public official committed to state service and not political ambition.

Along with the lieutenant governor, the House speaker is the other half of the Legislature's power couple. In their book on how the Texas speakership became a power in state and national politics, Patrick Cox and Michael Phillips write that the office tenure of Billy Clayton (1975-1983) began the transformation of the House's top post into a position of great political clout. The speakership under Tom Craddick (2003-2009) took the office to a near-dictatorial reign over the membership with a palace coup of Republicans and Democrats voting out "Auto" Craddick. The press referred to the Republican coup instigators as the "Gang of 11," who engineered the ouster of Craddick in favor of San Antonio Representative Joe Straus. In 2017 Straus was again elected by House members to continue as speaker for a fifth consecutive session despite the misgivings of some Tea Party R's.

What lieutenant governors and speakers have meant is different things to people inside and outside of Austin. For legislators, the Senate and House leaders have the power to reward and punish members based on their willingness to follow leadership directions. The old LBJ success adage for legislators of "to get along, you go along" sums up where members desiring to help the folks back home must be. When author (KB) was in the House, he and 15 other Democrats supported Republican Speaker Tom Craddick in spite of pleas from fellow D's and threats from trial lawyers to vote against Craddick in the House leadership race. KB's support for Craddick was based on the speaker's past help in getting things done for his working class Houston district.

For the Texas masses, the Senate and House leaders can make life better for them, but this rarely happens as the corporate agenda is the first order of business for the Legislature. It was the combination of legislative leaders and Governor Rick Perry who fought closing a business tax loophole in 2007 that allowed 4,000 corporations to escape paying $200 million a year in Texas taxes. Without the tax revenue, the Legislature balanced the budget through people cuts directed at teachers, students, children, and the poor. This action is all too typical in Austin where the Legislature sings the belt-tightening blues to the press and the public in both good and bad economic times.

While the leadership has control over the Senate and the House most of the time, there have been membership uprisings against those in charge. During the early 1940s, Price Daniel, a freshman representative, lead a group of colleagues known as "The Immortal 56" in a successful effort to block the enactment of a state sales tax. Most new members of legislatures are told by their senior colleagues to be "seen and not heard" during an apprenticeship period of a term or two, but this was not the case for Representative Daniel as he led the way in this early House tax revolt.

The "Dirty Thirty," a group of 30 Democrats and Republicans, called into question the ethical and leadership style of Speaker Gus Mutscher in 1971 during the time of the Sharpstown Bank scandal. The Texas Sharpstown scandal often would be linked with the 1973 Watergate national scandal in the public's mind as examples of government corruption at the highest political levels. With a cloud hanging over his head, Speaker Mutscher eventually decided to resign, and his House exit coincided with the departures of 76 representatives who were defeated for re-election in 1972. The new House elected a government reform speaker in Price Daniel Jr. who led a successful effort in passing new ethics laws.

In 1979 Lieutenant Governor Bill Hobby proposed moving the Texas presidential primary election from May to March. It was Hobby's hope that this change would allow conservative Democrats to vote for Republican-convert John Connally in the GOP March presidential primary, and then conservatives could return to their historic Democratic home in the May party balloting. The proposed Connally bill resulted in a group of liberal Democratic senators, known as the "Killer Bees," fleeing the Senate floor. The liberal flight denied the lieutenant governor the needed 21 members for a quorum that is required to conduct legislative business. Without a quorum, Hobby gave up on his primary change bill as the Bee sting turned out to be lethal to the Senate head.

Throughout the 1940s and the 1950s, a conservative coalition of Southern Democrats and Republicans controlled the U.S. Congress on proposals related to government spending, welfare programs, and labor union rights. During the 1980s and 1990s, a Texas conservative majority in the state House of most Democrats and Republicans held power over the chamber. Progressive Democrats, like Representative John Bryant, formed the House Study Group (HSG), and in the 1990s the Legislative Study Group (LSG) would become its liberal successor.

The HSG provided legislative research, pushed for rule changes, and organized progressives against the conservative agenda. With a new speaker Pete Laney in charge, the House Study Group was able to move Speaker Laney into adopting such democratic reforms as requiring the Calendars Committee to meet in public, insuring that bills be in members' offices 24 hours before consideration, and strengthening ethics rules leading to the creation of the Texas State Ethics Commission.

Taking the place of the HSG in 1994, the Legislative Study Group was a caucus of 70 liberal and moderate Democrats. Following the example of the Conservative Coalition, the LSG raised money to hire staff and researchers, published floor reports, and rallied members to oppose "bad" bills. It was the progressive study group that pushed the leadership into enacting the Children's Health Insurance Program (CHIP), a teacher pay raise, the first tax-free holiday, and the elimination of sales taxes on over-the-counter drugs.

The effective conservative legislative majority of traditional Democrats and Republicans would become a deep red majority in 2003 as the GOP took control of both the Senate and the House for the first time in 130 years. At the insistence of U.S. House Majority Leader Tom Delay, the Texas Legislature re-opened the approved congressional redistricting plan with the intention of redrawing new district lines to increase the number of Lone Star Republicans in Washington.

With the House leadership in Austin having the votes to make Delay's naked power grab a reality, the "Killer D's," a group of 52 Democrats, decided to run to Oklahoma. The flight of the Democrats meant that the House lacked a quorum or the required number of members present on the floor to proceed with any formal action. The Democratic tactic of quorum denial worked, and the House D's eventually came back to the Capitol as returning heroes to their supporters.

This lower chamber revolt of the Killer D's temporarily defeated Tom Delay's partisan gerrymandering plan, but Governor Rick Perry would add his political weight to the Hammer's muscle by calling a special session. The governor and the Republican legislative leaders would carry Delay's water, producing an unprecedented second redistricting plan. With the new lines in place, the red fix was in as four more Texas GOP congressmen and their votes would go off to Washington to help President George W. Bush in building "democratic" and "free" enterprise systems at home and abroad.

History of Corruption and Corporate Domination

A 2016 University of Texas poll by political consultant Leland Beatty found that roughly 60 percent of Texans believe that state government is corrupt. When it comes to the Senate and the House, citizens have good reason to hold this view, because the Legislature has a long and dark history of corruption and conflicts of interests.

It was a scene out of *Saturday Night Live* in 1989 when

millionaire Lonnie "Bo" Pilgrim was seen on the Texas Senate floor handing out $10,000 checks to members just prior to a key vote of importance to Pilgrim on workmen's compensation. The chicken magnet, founder of Pilgrim's Pride, defended his actions by calling the checks campaign contributions and not bribes. To most Texans, this explanation was for the birds.

From the 1970s to the 1990s, charges of corruption, indictments, and convictions swirled around three House speakers, and one lieutenant governor. The Sharpstown Bank scandal brought Speaker Gus Mutscher down as he was indicted and convicted of conspiracy to accept a lobbyist's bribe. Not charged formally with any crime, Lieutenant Governor Ben Barnes, the boy wonder of Texas politics, was guilty in the public's mind and left government in disgrace and defeat.

Two FBI undercover operations, ABSCAM and BRILAB, were carried out by Washington investigators in the 1970s to catch national and state legislators in the act of accepting bribes. The national sting operation, ABSCAM, resulted in U.S. Senator Harrison Williams, a New Jersey Democrat, and five U.S. representatives being found guilty of bribery and conspiracy charges with all six going to prison. BRILAB, the state sting operation, came close to bringing down Texas House Speaker Billy Wayne Clayton on bribery charges involving labor unions and government officials. Although indicted on accepting $5,000 with promises of $600,000 to follow, Clayton convinced a jury that he never intended to keep the money and was found not guilty in court. This sordid episode would undermine Clayton's standing in Austin and his tenure as a House leader.

Following Clayton's departure, Democrat Gib Lewis assumed the speakership and ended up going down the wrong side of the ethical road. Under numerous bribery charges and indictments in 1992, Speaker Lewis did not seek re-election as part of a plea bargain agreement associated with his misdemeanor conviction. In politics, saving face for an elected official and the government often lets people guilty as hell off the hook. This certainly was the case on October 10, 1973 when Vice-President Spiro Agnew agreed to resign the second highest office in the land. Agnew's resignation price was that the state of Maryland must drop its charges against him of accepting over $100,000 in kickbacks from state government contractors when he was governor. When President Richard Nixon would say a month later, "I am not a crook," not only was he wrong about himself but also about his VP.

While bribery and corruption are the lobbying mortal sins in Austin and Washington, lobbyists and legislators are committing venial sins against the public trust as a fact of political life. With the Texas Legislature only meeting every other year in regular session, the corporate lobby interests are working 24/7 to secure enormous influence over state government. Energy, insurance, and utility companies along with law firms spend huge amounts of money to receive favorable treatment from old returning friends and new "best" friends arriving in Austin.

Under state law, it is not illegal for business lobby groups to hire legislators to work on projects unrelated to official state business. In addition, corporate interests have a reputation of spending lavishly on dinners, receptions, special event tickets, hunting and fishing trips, and paying the expenses for senators and representatives to attend seminars in hot spots like Las Vegas, Honolulu, and San Diego. If this is not enough to win friends and influence votes, the wink and nod understanding of future employment as a consultant can be a strong inducement to stand with elites and not the masses.

Despite the call of the 2016 Republican presidential nominee to drain the Washington swamp of lobbyists, public affairs specialists have a constitutional right to represent the private interests of their clients before the U.S. Congress and the Texas Legislature. The First Amendment protects lobbying as long as interest group representatives adhere to the set rules and reporting practices. In the Lone Star State, legislators have little or no time to study and discuss issues so they have to rely on lobby information and research to frame bills. Interest groups do the heavy lifting of writing legislation that members can then introduce and claim as their own. To claim credit for another's work at the University of Texas will get a student thrown out of school as a plagiarist, but in the Legislature political credit claiming by members brings re-election, campaign contributions, and service awards. One author (BL) remembers sitting around a conference table in Austin six months before the start of a regular session and having an education lobbyist hand him a thick packet of school bills. After pro forma approval from teacher representatives, the lobbyist went out to locate friendly legislators to sponsor and to try to pass the bills into laws.

As the ghostwriters of bills, lobbyists pass off their legislative scripts to senators and representatives as part of the backstage maneuvering that goes on before the January opening curtain. Once the curtain is raised, the hired heads turn into locusts swarming the halls to meet and greet members and staffers, to fill committee rooms as a constant reminder that suits matter, to enter legislators' offices to press the flesh, and to look down from the gallery section known around the Capitol as the owner's box.

In making a final comment about the history of corruption and corporate domination in Texas, the tragedy is not about the member crooks who are disgraced, defeated, indicted, fined, and jailed, but about an unreformed state government system that continues to remain in place. The real government tragedy in Texas is that economic elites and their rented legislators participate in an elaborate political Ponzi scheme in which the masses end up with broken promises and little of policy value for their participation and support of a fraudulent system.

Concluding Remarks

The Legislature is the strongest among the three weak formal branches of Texas government. Time is the greatest limitation on senators and representatives who effectively have just 62 days to complete two years of state work. Differences can be found among those willing to serve in the Senate and the House, and members' work styles and modes of behavior can vary from the "organization man" to the "delegate." The lieutenant governor and the speaker are the power couple of the first branch of government, but membership challenges to the leadership have developed in the past over policy and political differences. While corruption is part of the institution's history, the more relevant fact is the extent of corporate and elite domination over the bicameral body at the expense of good government and the public interest.

Works Noted

Bailey, Stephen Kemp. 1950. *Congress Makes a Law*. New York: Vintage Books.

Squire Peverill and Gary Moncrief. 2015. *State Legislatures Today*. Lanham, MD: Rowman & Littlefield.

Goodwin, George. 1970. *The Little Legislatures*. Amherst, MA: The University of Massachusetts Press.

Barber, James David. 1965. *The Lawmakers*. New Haven, CT: Yale University Press.

Green, Mark J., 1972. *Who Runs Congress?*. New York: Bantam Books.

Davidson, Roger H. 1969. *The Role of the Congressman*. New York: Pegasus.

Hobby, Bill. 2010. *How Things Really Work*. Austin: Briscoe Center.

Cox, Patrick and Michael Phillips. 2010. *The House Will Come to Order*. Austin: University of Texas Press.

CHAPTER EIGHT

GOVERNORS IN TEXAS

"A Texas Governor has only two happy days: the day he is inaugurated and the day he retires," Governor Joseph Draper Sayers said about his 1899-1903 office experience. The statement of Sayers could not have been more different from what George W. Bush told his successor Rick Perry "that being Governor of Texas was the best job in the world."

For good or bad, the Texas governorship like the American presidency has been an evolving office depending on the occupant and the times. The "first" executives of both the state and national offices are thought of quite differently in history. It is probably true that only dead Americans are unable to identify the first U.S. president, but many Texas history buffs are stumped when asked to name the first governor of the Lone Star State. It is not Sam Houston, number eight on the list, but James Pinckney Henderson. Elected in 1845, Henderson will never be confused with George Washington as a chief executive.

While American historians rate Washington as the second greatest president behind Abraham Lincoln and in front of Franklin

Roosevelt, Texas historians have relegated Henderson to the status of a footnote in their books. During his single two-year term, Governor Henderson was absent from office for seven months in 1846 to lead a band of Lone Star volunteers to fight for American imperialism in a war against Mexico. What red-blooded governor would not want to head an army of *"Los Diablos Tejanos,"* or Texas Rangers, to fight Mexicans in order to settle old political scores and to take the territories of New Mexico and California away from the mother country?

The Constitution and the Governor

The main purpose in writing a new state constitution in 1875, as was pointed out in Chapter Two, was to restrict the powers of state government. This purpose was achieved throughout the 17 articles with Article IV covering the executive department being a strong check against gubernatorial power. In their indictment of the all-powerful executive, the constitutional framers had Republican Reconstruction Governor Edmund Davis in mind, whose authoritarian actions they swore would never happen again. How did the constitutional authors go about insuring that there would be no future despotic Davises in government? The answer lies in the details of Article IV creating an emasculated executive.

After the 1875 framers got done with the office of governor, Richard Coke and his successors were put in the formal position of all hat, no cattle. Under the 1866 and 1869 Constitutions, the authority allowing Governor Davis to rule in the fashion of a dictatorial leader would end. What government powers deemed necessary, the 1875 authors would assign to the legislative branch.

This external assault on the strong governor model would be combined with an internal attack on the unchecked executive that the framers achieved through both the reduction and the separation of powers. The constitution writers cut future governors down to size by shortening the office term from four years to two, by prohibiting them from holding any other public or private office, by forbidding the state executive from practicing any profession for salary or profit, and by specifying the duties of the position in limiting detail. This reduction of the governor's office from what it had been would bring a smile today from Jenny Craig. As will be shown later in the chapter, a governor desiring to be more than a department store mannequin would not be happy over this new Texas shrunken head.

Along with the reduction of office power under Article IV, the 1875 framers approved a plural executive system by taking power away from the governor, a single executive, and dispersing it into the hands of other executive officials. The current Texas Constitution established an executive power sharing system by having the governor, lieutenant governor, attorney general, comptroller of public accounts, treasurer, and commissioner of the general land office established as independent offices. An additional executive office, commissioner of agriculture, was created through legislative action in 1907. The authority of these offices and the officials in charge derive from the constitution and law and not the governor which is good for everyone but the governor.

This plural executive system weakens any governor's authority and political standing. As indicated in Chapter Seven, the lieutenant governor's office may be the most powerful position in state government. Within the national government, the equivalent post is not the powerless vice-presidency but the position of Senate majority leader. Within the federal government, the president heads a single executive system of 15 cabinet departments with the department heads serving at the pleasure of the chief executive. This is not the case in Texas where independence and competition can make life miserable for a governor with an uncooperative attorney general or a stone walling comptroller. If Presidents George H.W. Bush or Bill Clinton had been unhappy with a treasury or defense secretary, they could simply ask for the secretary's immediate resignation.

The famous Trump phrase, "You're fired!" could not work for Governor Bill Clements when he clashed with Attorney General Mark White in the late 1970s. This clash should come as no surprise as Republican Clements and Democrat White represented different partisan and government outlooks. Imagine how uncomfortable President Ronald Reagan would have felt had someone like Robert Kennedy been the attorney general during his administration. Fortunately for Reagan, he was able to choose his longtime friend and party loyalist Edwin Meese to serve as AG.

From the standpoint of checking power, the Texas plural executive structure works well, but it can bring pain and suffering to a governor trying to lead and to administer state government. During the first term of Governor Clements, he battled with Attorney General White over the interpretation of their roles and offices. The two were forced to co-exist in the Texas executive branch as each was elected by the voters in 1978. The attorney general was able to rid himself of the governor when he beat Clements in the 1982 gubernatorial election, but the mano-a-mano contest would not end there as candidate Clements defeated Governor White in his 1986 re-election bid.

For voters tired of both Clements and White, 1990 brought relief when Governor Clements chose not to run for re-election, and White would lose the Democratic gubernatorial nomination to Ann Richards. The potential for internal party conflict also existed as Democratic State Treasurer Ann Richards and Democratic Attorney General Jim Maddox faced off against each other for their party's 1990 nomination for governor. Known as the "Junkyard Dog" of Texas politics, Maddox ran a bruising nomination campaign of personal attacks against Lady Richards with allegations of drug use and hints of a gay lifestyle.

The plural executive system has been partially responsible for not only Democrats eating their own, but 2014 Republicans became killer sharks in the GOP nomination pool for lieutenant governor. Agriculture Commissioner Todd Staples and Land Commissioner

Jerry Patterson got into the ring against each other as each tried to knock off the incumbent David Dewhurst. While Dewhurst finished ahead of Staples and Patterson in the candidate field, he lost the GOP primary runoff to State Senator Dan Patrick.

Who Can Be Governor?

It used to be said that any boy in Texas can grow up to be governor, and the legal requirements of having to be at least thirty, a US citizen, and five years of state residency before the election would seem, especially if girls are included, to hold out hope for all. With the three formal requirements of Article IV making twelve million possible governors, the reality is quite different for the odds of the average person becoming the next governor are next to zero.

What political scientists have shown is there are any number of informal requirements needed if a candidate is serious about being the state chief executive. These informal points have been developed over time by looking at those who made it to the top spot and their shared characteristics. Political profilers say that a Texas governor should be white, Anglo, male, and Christian. The only exceptions to these four points were the two women executives Miriam Ferguson and Ann Richards; the day for an African-American, Hispanic, or non-Christian has not yet arrived in the Lone Star State.

Along with the unstated requirements of race, ethnicity, gender, and religion, other background factors like age, wealth, education, occupation, and ideology can be added to the composite picture of candidates who realistically can expect to become governor. Many past officeholders have been 45 to 55, persons of means, lawyers and businessmen, college-educated, and political conservatives. Some governor exceptions to these general rules were 33-year-old Dan Moody, hillbilly band leader "Pappy" O'Daniel, and the most liberal of all Texas executives James Allred.

In an attempt to go further in understanding the gubernatorial selection process, the work of Joseph Schlesinger, author of *Ambition in Politics*, is invaluable. His ambition theory suggests that rising to the top executive state or national office generally goes to those individuals able to move up the political ladder from lower offices. What Schlesinger looks at is the prior governmental position held by a candidate who makes it to the top. For presidents, the three career launching pads to the Oval Office have been the vice-presidency, a state governorship, and the U.S. Senate with the VP office being the number one political road to the White House.

While presidents have gotten to the White House from three main tracks, Texas governors over the past 60 years have followed a different set of trails to the executive mansion. State government insiders have used the offices of: Attorney General; Greg Abbott in 2014, Lieutenant Governor; Rick Perry in 2002, State Treasurer; Ann Richards in 1990, and the Texas House; Dolph Briscoe in 1972. Winning the highest executive office has gone to some candidates who were Austin outsiders, such as John Connally in 1962 and William Clements in 1978. Connally and Clements held prior positions in the Pentagon in Washington. In 1994, George W. Bush, son of a former president and part-owner of the Texas Rangers baseball team, won the office over Governor Richards.

In looking at the informal requirements and prior career experiences, it can be said that the possible pool of millions eligible to run for governor every four years is drained to a handful of serious candidates that have any chance of winning. Even though he was a multimillionaire, Tony Sanchez's prospects of victory in 2002 were not helped by his ethnicity, nor were the prospects of Wendy Davis in 2014 given a boost by her gender. Breakthroughs do occur as witnessed by the presidential victories of African-American Barack Obama in 2008 and government outsider Donald Trump in 2016, but like "Hail Mary" passes in football the success rate for unconventional candidates is low.

Powers of the Governor

Compared to the formal powers of all 50 state governors, political scientist Joseph Schlesinger rated the Texas governor in last place, a general without an army. Following the ratification of the 1972 constitutional amendment extending the governor's term to four years, the Schlesinger power rating in the 1980s moved the Texas executive into the 49th spot. It is no wonder that Fred Gantt, author of *The Chief Executive in Texas*, ends his book by writing about Lone Star governors with the words that the "Chief Executive of Texas under the existing laws, might more accurately be thought of as the "Chief Persuader in Texas."

While state-government experts do not mistake the weak constitutional powers of the Texas persuader with the strong powers possessed by governors in Massachusetts and New York, the Texas Constitution does assign five formal powers to the governor similar to those of the American president. As Clinton Rossiter once said of presidents, the U.S. Constitution requires a president to wear a number of hats at once or to play a variety of roles, as the state charter expects a governor to be a political shapeshifter.

Rossiter's hats or roles applied to state governors might be thought of as the five chiefs: chief of state, chief executive, chief legislator, chief administrator, and commander in chief. As chief of state, the governor is the human symbol of Texas presenting a public face to state and national audiences. It was the swagger of George W. Bush that played so well in Texas, while out-of-state reactions were mixed. Ann Richards' humor and celebrity made her a national figure, but at home many found her to be a bit much.

Along with representing the state at ceremonial events, such as Governor Rick Perry flipping the coin at the Texas Bowl game, the governor acting as chief of state appoints the military head of the Texas State Guard and has the authority to commute prison sentences and to stay executions. Despite international pressure in 1998, Governor George W. Bush refused to stay the execution of Karla Faye Tucker, the first woman to be killed by Texas since the Civil War. While the Bush decision received criticism outside of the state, most Texans agreed with the governor in not sparing the life of an axe murderer who became a born-again Christian in prison. As the first citizen of Texas, a governor can use his bully pulpit to try to persuade residents to agree with his viewpoint as Governor Dolph Briscoe did in 1975 with his opposition to constitutional revision.

The chief executive role is the second hat that governors wear. In this role, governors are expected to see that the laws are faithfully executed. Although the attorney general is the top legal officer of the state, it is left to the governor to oversee that laws are administered properly within the state bureaucracy. Failure to do so can lead to the extreme penalty of impeachment and removal from office. Within the federal government, two presidents, Andrew Johnson and Bill Clinton, were impeached or indicted by the U.S. House, but both were found not guilty in Senate trials. The one near certain presidential impeachment, conviction, and possible jailing would have been Richard Nixon who avoided this fate by resigning his office and receiving a presidential pardon from Gerald Ford. In Texas, Governor James "Pa" Ferguson did not have Nixon's luck as he resigned from office, only to have the House proceed to impeach him in 1917 on 21 articles. The state Senate found him guilty on ten counts with the most serious being his misuse of public funds and the acceptance of a $150,000 bribe.

When Governor Ann Richards felt the State Insurance Commission was not carrying out its responsibilities to consumers in 1992, she exerted her chief executive authority by publicly calling out the commissioners. In 1993 Richards was able to get the Legislature to abolish the commission and to replace it with a new Texas Department of Insurance.

It was Clifton McCleskey, author of *The Government and Politics of Texas*, who wrote that "the heart of a Governor's job lies in legislation." As a chief legislator, governors derive a number of powers from Article IV including message power, special session power, and veto power. It was in her first State of the State message that Governor Richards laid out a vision for a "New Texas" government, open to all, diverse in makeup, and ethical in its operations.

With only 140 days in a regular session that meets every other year, the Texas House and Senate must rely on the executive's authority to send the Legislature back to work. During the twentieth century, governors called special 30-day sessions to deal with matters of taxation, appropriations, road bonds, prison reform, social welfare issues, and teacher salaries. Governor Dan Moody holds the record number of five special session calls during the life of the 41st Texas Legislature. This special session power of governors can be used to allow the House and Senate to complete unfinished work or to persuade legislators to act the executive's way or they will be forced into a 30-day detention period in Austin. It was no surprise to political observers when Governor Greg Abbott called his first special session at the end of the 85th Legislature. There was a big surprise, however, by the crazy number of items—20 for legislators to consider during the July-August 2017 special meeting.

One of the most publicized special sessions occurred in the summer of 2013 as a result of Senator Wendy Davis' successful filibuster against a highly restrictive anti-abortion bill. With the pro-choice Davis able to run out the clock of the regular session and block the bill, Governor Rick Perry, an abortion-is-murder proponent, called a special session to get the most restrictive abortion bill in the nation established as Texas law. While Perry overrode the Davis talk-a-thon, the U.S. Supreme Court in 2016 would override the governor and the legislature by declaring HB2 to be unconstitutional in the case of the *Whole Woman's Health v. Hellerstedt.*

While the message and special session powers are important

to governors as legislative chiefs, many political scientists feel the executive veto of a legislative bill is their greatest power. It is not often that the names of Franklin Roosevelt and Rick Perry would be listed together, but the two share a similar record in their respective government arenas. Among presidents, FDR holds the record of 635 for the most vetoes, while Perry is the record holder among Texas governors with 292. During his first legislative session, Governor Perry sent shockwaves among legislators, who had already left Austin for home, when he vetoed 82 bills in an action that became known as the Father's Day massacre around the state capital.

In looking at the governor's veto power, this power includes something presidents lack which is the line-item veto power. The item veto is a formidable executive tool applying only to appropriations or spending bills. What a governor can do is to approve or disapprove singular parts within a comprehensive or multi-part legislative bill. Within the federal government, presidents have no authority to do this as they are forced to approve or disapprove bills in their entirety. For a short time, a Republican Congress provided Democratic President Bill Clinton with the item veto power through the legislative process, only to have the U.S. Supreme Court strike down the law as unconstitutional in 1996. One of the authors (BL) remembers when Governor Bill Clements exercised a line-item veto to kill a special funding provision for North Harris County College. The NHCC funds were included within a Christmas tree bill that saw Governor Clements play Scrooge as he took the North Harris ornament off the tree with his line-item power.

In addition to the governor being a chief of state, chief executive, and chief legislator, his fourth office role is chief administrator. In wearing this hat, the governor's main power stems from the authority to make appointments to over 200 state boards and commissions. Brian McCall, author of *The Powers of the Texas Governor*, believes that the appointment power is the most significant executive power. Without question, Governor Perry has been the most effective in this role as his long tenure allowed him to select over 7,500 appointees to the state bureaucracy in his 14 year tenure.

With staggered terms for state administrators and up to six years in office, every administrator was a Perry pick midway through the governor's time in Austin. For his last six years, it was Perry time all the time as the Republican chief put a variety of party loyalists, political friends, and campaign contributors into state posts. With his ability to remake the face of Texas government in his own ideological image, the man from Paint Creek would earn the name "Caudillo" governor, or strong-man leader, from Richard Parker, author of *Lone Star Nation*. This Perry phenomenon meant that crony capitalism and corporate welfare ruled in Austin, a big win for the rich and well-connected but a major loss for the people of Texas.

The final constitutional role of the governor is commander in chief (CINC) of the Texas State Guard, which along with the Texas Army and Texas Air National Guard make up the state military force. As CINC, Governor Perry appointed General John F. Nichols as the state top military commander in 2011. The job of the state guard is to assist the citizens of Texas in disaster relief as guardsmen did during Hurricane Ike in 2008 and the Bastrop Forest Fires in 2014.

Political controversies have sometimes swirled around the Texas military as questions have been raised about George W. Bush as a uniformed member and Gregg Abbott's actions as a chief commander. For Bush, a Texas Air National Guard pilot in the 1970s, both his admission and his service record came under press investigations. After W became a presidential candidate in 2000, *60 Minutes* ran a report about Bush's absences from duty based on what turned out to be bogus documents. CBS would fire newsman Dan Rather over his broadcast errors, but questions remained about political strings being pulled to get him into the guard and over his service time while in Alabama.

As the Texas commander in chief, Governor Abbott's 2015

directive to Texas Guard General Jake Berry, to monitor the U.S. military exercise "Jade Helm," ended up putting Abbott and Texas paranoia over the federal government on full display in the comic strip *Doonesbury*. Strip creator Gary Trudeau and late night TV comics had a field day over Abbott's directive and Texans who thought the U.S. training exercise might be the start of a federal government takeover of the Lone Star State.

Types of Governors

American political scientists classify presidents into two main categories first identified with Theodore Roosevelt (TR) and William Howard Taft. The TR or strong executive wants to exert assertive leadership, while the Taftian or weak president chooses a more managerial approach to governing. The United States has had both "great" strong types, Abraham Lincoln and Franklin Roosevelt, and major strong "failures," Lyndon Johnson and Richard Nixon. Weak or successful managerial presidents of note have been George Washington and Dwight Eisenhower with James Buchanan and Herbert Hoover being the worst of the second type.

Like presidents, governors have been placed under the political science microscope over the years. In his study of Texas chief executives, Fred Gantt found six different types of governors from the time of James Pinckney Henderson (1846-1847) through Price Daniel (1957-1963). Based on a number of other accounts and the authors' observations, the Gantt typology will be updated for post-Daniel executives from John Connally to Greg Abbott. The original classification of Gantt's Texas governors included: the strong leader, the figurehead, the man of the people, the grafter, the showman, and the reformer.

Traits of strong leaders include knowledge, intelligence, attractiveness, courage, and independence. It is the view of Gantt that Allan Shivers (1949-1957) represented this type. James Anderson, author of *Texas Politics: An Introduction*, agrees with Gantt and refers to Shivers as an "aggressive leader." In more recent times, it is clear that John Connally (1963-1969), citied by journalist Paul Burka of *Texas Monthly* as the "greatest twentieth-century governor" and the "architect of modern Texas," was another strong leader. Connally's leadership was in the areas of higher education, tourism, and economic development. It would be impossible not to include Rick Perry (2000-2015), Parker's Caudillo, in this group. It is a reasonable bet that future scholars will put Perry through the same historical shredder as Johnson and Nixon with the governor coming out as a strong leader gone wrong.

The polar opposite of the strong leader is the figurehead or Gantt's second kind of executive. The figurehead is a weak, colorless, gubernatorial zero. The classic example here was Miriam "Ma" Ferguson (1925-1927, 1933-1935), who played the "dummy" sitting on her impeached husband Pa's lap as he called the shots. While Dolph Briscoe (1973-1979) was his own man, his do-nothing philosophy resembling Calvin Coolidge puts him into this category. It can be said of Briscoe that he promised the people of Texas next to nothing and delivered well on his promise.

Classifying in-office executives can be a tricky business, but it has been done and will sometimes backfire over time as has been the case with President Harry Truman. Looking at Gregg Abbott (2015) as a first term governor, his place appears to be settling in as a Briscoe-like figure willing to let others lead and to toe the Tea Party line. In his book, *Broken But Unbowed*, Abbott's simple message is how evil the federal government is and how good the people of Texas are. The last executive to express the public's goodness was President Jimmy Carter who wanted a government as good as the American people. Unlike Carter, Abbott seems to have missed the point that the government of Texas is good for elites but bad for the masses.

For the first half of the twentieth century, Larry Sabato generalized that many of the nation's governors were "Good-time

Charlies," a mixed group of courthouse politicians, gladhanders, and men of modest achievements. This "average" state executive coincides with Gantt's third type or the man of the people governor. Governor Sul Ross (1887-1897) and Charles Culberson (1895-1899) are nineteenth century examples of men "who have no ideas as to what a governor can do, and hence follow a policy of drifting and opportunism." Gantt brands the majority of Texas executives as type threes or the proverbial "C" college student who puts in some course effort and ends up with a 2.0. Among post-1962 officeholders, the best third type example is Bill Clements (1979-1983, 1987-1991), who ranks as a middle of the pack governor with no lasting achievements. Praised for administrative skills, Clements, according to James Anderson, has as his "prized accomplishment" that he slowed the growth of state government, hardly the basis for a future Broadway play.

The grafter governor is the fourth executive type representing someone who has committed office malfeasance or exhibited scandalous behavior. Despite the Texas image of the wheeler-dealer politician without legal scruples, the Lone Star executive record looks pure in comparison to a state like Illinois where four of the last eight governors have gone to prison. The impeached "Pa" Ferguson (1915-1917) is an easy choice here as he was forced out of office for crimes committed in Austin. Along with Ferguson, Preston Smith (1969-1973) bears inclusion as a grafter due to his association with the 1971 Sharpstown Bank scandal. Sharpstown, the Texas Watergate, is the greatest political scandal in state history. This caper involved a stock fraud scheme and bribery at the highest levels of government. Although no formal charges were brought against Governor Smith, he did profit personally from selling stock shares and was an unindicted co-conspirator in the messy arrangement. Smith's connection to Frank Sharp, found guilty of violating federal bribery laws, ended the governor's political career.

The showman or celebrity governor is Gantt's fifth executive type. This type loves the office for the public stage and the large audiences that go with it. In his book on presidential personality types, James David Barber writes about passive-positive executives, like Ronald Reagan, who derive great satisfaction from being in the White House as it fills a need for public love and affection. Gantt's showman is related to Barber's passive-positive who probably enjoys campaigning more than governing. Governor W. Lee O'Daniel (1939-1941) was a master showman with his hillbilly band and radio broadcasting skills. Of governors since Connally, Ann Richards (1991-1995) fits this pattern of a political celebrity with her wit, stage-presence, and Hollywood star quality. Her new Texas administration based on breaking up the good old boy network and opening up government to those left out in the past was strong on symbols but light on substance.

The last of the six governor types is the reformer. Executive reformers are bent on fixing state policy problems or addressing an unmet public need. Fred Gantt identifies Governors James Hogg (1891-1895) for effecting railroad reform, Dan Moody (1927-1931) for revamping the prison system, and James Allred (1935-1939) for championing social welfare programs as Texas reformers. At the presidential level, Franklin Roosevelt and Ronald Reagan might be cited as the two greatest twentieth century reformers with their "big" and "no" government approaches to domestic policy.

Among governors over the past 50 years, Mark White (1983-1987) and George W. Bush (1995-2000) would seem to align with Gantt's reformer. It is White who should be remembered as the education governor for his work to improve public schools. Many governors before and after White have talked about education, but he produced substantive changes in school funding, teacher pay, instructional accountability, and the "no-pass-no-play" policy. This last change so angered high school football coaches, concerned over losing players over poor grades, that they organized a political action committee to stop White's re-election in 1986.

Like White, Governor Bush was a reform executive. Bush

certainly qualifies as an "effective" officeholder using Barbara Kellerman's definition found in her book on presidents. For Kellerman, an effective executive lays out his stated goals and is able to achieve much of what he sets out to do. The author of *The Political Presidency* lists Lyndon Johnson and Ronald Reagan as effective modern presidents. In Texas, Bush listed four reforms in his 1994 gubernatorial race in the policy areas of welfare, education, tort litigation, and juvenile crime. What candidate Bush promised on the campaign trail was delivered in office with the support of top legislative Democrats like Bob Bullock and Pete Laney.

Governors and Mass Lives

Texas governors from James Pinckney Henderson to Greg Abbott have talked the "talk" of being for the people, but few have walked the "walk" to take the steps needed to back up their populist rhetoric. While a 2016 national debate took place over whether "Black or Blue or All Lives Matter," Texas history has shown that with few exceptions governors oversee a state where just "Elite Lives Matter." Among all chief executives, the one common link between Democrats and Republicans and liberals and conservatives is the understanding and the acceptance of a state power structure where elites matter most and then there are the masses.

What has been witnessed from Texas liberal governors, like James Allred and Ann Richards, is a cautious and pragmatic course in an attempt to bring something positive for citizens without offending the rich and the powerful. Conservative governors, like Dolph Briscoe and Rick Perry, have played defense and offense for economic elites in order to keep the power structure intact and to enhance their political standing.

In looking at Governors Allred, Richards, Briscoe, and Perry, what have their actions or inactions meant for the people without wealth or status? Allred and Richards represent two strands of liberal Democratic philosophy: labor liberalism and social liberalism. Elected as a conservative in 1934, Allred set aside his traditionalism to embrace FDR's New Deal programs including state measures for old age assistance, teacher retirement programs, and labor union rights.

The Great Depression may have turned Governor Allred into a convert to labor-liberalism, but for Ann Richards there was no liberal conversion experience as she stood for social liberalism throughout her public life. As a champion for civil rights, Richards worked diligently on equality issues for women, African-Americans, and Hispanics. Her fight for minority rights in the 1990s was a big deal in a state where the tradition of male, white, and Anglo supremacy was the Lone Star way.

Did Allred and Richards make a difference for the Texas masses? The short answer is "Yes." Did their actions bring about a political revolution in the state? The one-word answer is "No." Absent a major social movement that would turn Texas into Denmark, the best nonelites can hope for are the types of institutional changes that Allred and Richards brought in the economic and social rights areas.

The populist ideas of today calling for higher wages for workers, free college tuition for students, and health care for all are met with reaction of the top one percent that these proposals are too costly and will kill the economy. Elite opposition to any "Mass Lives Matter" movement for economic justice will come from the perceived beliefs of the wealthy that gains for average Texans will come at their expense. There is no way to allay upper-class fears here, because their perceptions are not totally wrong. To improve mass lives will require a greater contribution from the wealthy to finance public-private initiatives to bring about a better Texas for all.

It is at this time that public leaders must confront the state powers that be with the choice faced by the wealthy in America during the 1930s. Although thought of as a traitor to his class,

President Roosevelt saved U.S. capitalism for the nation's elites by transforming the economic system that resulted in improving the lives of the masses without destroying the class structure. FDR's New Deal programs meant a better life and future for millions of people with the coming of social welfare capitalism replacing the old laissez faire market system of the 1920s. The "how" to bring this transformation about will be taken up in the last chapter of the book.

While Allred and Richards brought some wins for working people, Governors Briscoe and Perry acted as agents for the well off in life. After the Sharpstown scandal, Dolph Briscoe won office and proceeded through his absences from Austin and his executive inaction to reinforce the status quo: good for elites but bad for masses. Had the wealthy Anglo rancher stopped there, he would have been no different than most Democratic governors before him in offering platitudes about the rich history of Texas and the greatness of its people to overcome any obstacle.

In his 1974 reelection campaign, Briscoe decided to act, however, against an emerging Hispanic political movement, La Raza Unida, whose leaders Ramsey Muniz and Jose Angel Gutierrez tried to awaken Mexican-Americans to take power through voting and protesting. Perhaps for business and certainly for political reasons, the Uvalde multimillionaire governor ran a racist, smear campaign against La Raza Party candidates. Briscoe's allegations about the Valley becoming a "Little Cuba," and his suggestions that Chicano leaders were connected to Fidel Castro were statements that only a birther like Donald Trump would believe.

Many low income Anglos voted for Briscoe in 1972 and 1974 as they saw him as their champion against the perceived threat of Republicans and the brown masses. While poor whites may have received some satisfaction from the Briscoe win, his victory meant little improvement for their lives. It is commonplace for Texas elected officials to stiff the people and to roll out the red carpet for the rich. How have establishment executives pulled off this double play? First, political leaders can do nothing for which the *Seinfeld* TV show and the Briscoe administration were famous for. Second, an elected leader, like Rick Perry, can make policy decisions clearly benefitting elites and not the masses.

While Jerry Seinfeld's nothingness was funny, Briscoe's nothingness was no laughing matter for millions of people. The Democrat's failure to speak out for a new constitution in 1974 and then to come out against the 1975 propositions contributed to Texas losing a chance to modernize and democratize its political system. The governor's false claim that a new constitution meant a state income tax made the difference for some voters. The sad irony for the masses is that an income tax would be beneficial to them and not economic elites, who prefer to go their own private way in areas like education, recreation, neighborhood security, transportation, and health care. Throughout Texas history, the upper class has never allowed the sin of greed to get in its way of pursuing more wealth and greater profits.

While Dolph Briscoe's inaction had the effect of meaning more for elites and less for the masses, Governor Rick Perry's actions meant much more for elites and much less for the masses. During his long tenure, Perry established himself as the Texas king of corporate welfare. His support from 2002 to 2014 of the Chapter 313 economic program meant over $6 billion in tax credits for businesses in what Professor Nathan Jensen of the University of Texas has called a "waste of taxpayer dollars" that could have been used for needed citizen services. The governor's version of crony capitalism meant a $500 million windfall for businesses with few strings attached in return for a promise of strengthening the state economy and bringing new jobs into the state. Perry's handouts of $40 million to Toyota, $21 million to Apple, and $12 million to Chevron through his Texas Enterprise Fund were expensive gifts for corporations with little to show for it at the end of the day. Under the economic guise of a rising tide lifting all boats, the governor's programs, much like those of President Ronald Reagan, simply showed that the tide created raised many yachts while sinking many rowboats.

In taking care of the have-mores and haves, Rick Perry ended up doing harm to the have-somes and have-nots by leading the way on public school spending cuts, college tuition deregulation, child health insurance reductions, jobless benefits curtailments, and Medicaid extension refusals. Perry's hits on the lives of K-12 kids, college students, poor children, the unemployed, and the uninsured brought misery to the Texas masses. It would seem that the governor's professed commitment to his Christian faith never got in the way of his unshakable belief in the lords of commerce.

Concluding Remarks

Among all state governors, the Texas chief executive remains among the weakest. This situation of an emasculated executive stems from the 1876 Constitution and the plural executive arrangement. For any citizen wanting to be governor, a number of informal requirements and prior office experiences can enhance a candidate's winning chances. Once in office, a governor exercises five powers that align with five chief roles from chief of state to commander in chief. While presidents are divided historically into strong and weak categories, Fred Gantt identified six types of governors from the strong leader to the reformer. Throughout Texas history, all governors have had to deal with the power reality of elite dominance over government, but some, like James Allred and Ann Richards, attempted to improve mass lives, while others, like Dolph Briscoe and Rick Perry, only made mass lives worse.

Works Noted

Schlesinger, Joseph A. 1966. *Ambition in Politics.* Chicago: Rand McNally.

Gantt, Fred. 1964. *The Chief Executive in Texas.* Austin: University of Texas Press.

Rossiter, Clinton. 1960. *The American Presidency.* New York: Harcourt, Brace & World.

McCleskey, Clifton. 1963. *The Government and Politics of Texas.* Boston: Little, Brown and Company.

McCall, Brian. 2009. *The Power of the Texas Governor.* Austin: University of Texas Press.

Parker, Richard. 2014. *Lonestar Nation.* New York: Pegasus Books.

Anderson, James E. 1992. *Texas Politics.* New York: Harper Collins Publishers.

Abbott, Greg. *Broken But Unbowed.* 2016. New York: Threshold Editions.

Sabato, Larry. 1983. *Goodbye to Good-Time Charlie.* Washington, D.C.: CQ Press.

Barber, James David. 1972. *The Presidential Character.* Englewood Cliffs, N.J.: Prentice Hall.

Kellerman, Barbara. 1984. *The Political Presidency.* New York: Oxford University Press.

CHAPTER NINE

Judiciary and Bureaucracy in Texas

In "Federalist No. 78," Alexander Hamilton wrote in 1788 that the national judiciary would be the weakest among the three formal branches of government. Hamilton's third or "least dangerous" branch did not have the legislature's power over the purse or the executive's command of the sword. While the U.S. court system was intended to be a political lightweight among the heavyweight Congress and the middleweight presidency, the bureaucracy considered today to be a fourth or informal government branch was set up to be under the thumb of the two elected branches. Both the American judiciary and bureaucracy and the Texas judiciary and bureaucracy have not turned out as their constitutional and legislative creators planned. What this means is that magistrates and bureaucrats have developed into powerful political players from their modest origins.

In Chapter Two on Texas Constitutions, a comparative point was made about the similar institutional arrangement from first to third of the legislative, executive, and judicial articles within the national and state constitutions. Neither U.S. Article IV nor Texas Article VI covers the bureaucracy, which is why large government organizations like the United States Defense Department and the Texas Education Agency are classified as public parts of an informal fourth branch. The courts and the bureaucracy will be the subject of Chapter Nine as we will focus on the impact these institutions have on the lives and fortunes of the elites and masses of Texas. It will be our contention that federal courts and agencies have brought some hope to the people over the years, but that both the state judiciary and the bureaucracy generally have meant high hopes and realized expectations for the haves and little hope and unanswered prayers for the have-nots.

Two Types and Five Tiers

In the area of the law, there are two main types or recognized categories: civil and criminal. Civil law deals with private disputes over family issues, property questions, and contractual obligations. Criminal law addresses areas in which the state can punish unlawful behavior like property theft, personal assault, and murder.

Because of the unified legal system, the U.S. Supreme Court handles both civil and criminal law cases which is the practice for the highest state courts everywhere but in Texas and Oklahoma. For the Lone Star State and its neighbor, the separation of civil cases from criminal cases results in a two-headed court structure. In Texas, the Supreme Court is the highest civil court, while the Court of Criminal Appeals is the end of the state line for criminal cases. Losing parties in the two top courts have an opportunity to appeal to the U.S. Supreme Court for review of a Texas ruling. It is within the first 18 words of Article V of the Texas Constitution that establish the dual judiciary by vesting power "in one Supreme Court, and in a (Criminal) Court of Appeals."

Below the top tier of the Supreme Court and the Court of Criminal Appeals can be found four lower tiers: Courts of Appeal, District Courts, County-Level Courts, and the basement benches of Municipal and Justice-of-the-Peace Courts. The five-tiered Texas system makes it the Mount Everest among the national and state judiciaries. The federal judiciary is made up of one Supreme Court, 13 Circuit Courts of Appeal, and 94 District Courts. Like the U.S. system, the California court structure has three levels. The Florida state system, however, comes closer to the Texas configuration, but it falls one tier short with its Supreme Court, District Courts of Appeal, Circuit Courts, and County Courts.

Like the U.S. Supreme Court (SCOTUS), the Texas Supreme Court carries great prestige and importance. Each court today has a chief justice and eight associate justices but neither started out that way. Originally, the American Supreme Court began with Chief Justice John Jay and five associate judges. The first session of the Texas Supreme Court in 1876 had Oran Roberts as its chief and two associates George Moore and Robert Gould.

Over the years the makeup of each Supreme Court would evolve, and members other than white Anglo men would eventually take their seats on the top courts. For SCOTUS, the first African-American, female, and Hispanic judges would be Thurgood Marshall (1967), Sandra Day O'Connor (1981), and Sonia Sotomayor (2009). Presidents Lyndon Johnson, Ronald Reagan, and Barack Obama deserve credit for making these historic appointments. Governors Bill Clements, Mark White, and George W. Bush would appoint the first woman Ruby Kless Sondock (1982), the first Hispanic Raul A. Gonzalez (1984), and the first African-American Wallace Jefferson (2001) to the Texas Supreme Court.

While Texas has the tallest court system in America with its five tiers, this has not meant that the Lone Star State has the most just system. Kyle Cheek and Anthony Champagne, authors of *Judicial Politics in Texas*, have characterized the state court system as a mixture of "money, partisanship, failed reform efforts, and sometimes corruption." Political controversies have swirled around the Texas judiciary over two features not found in the U.S. court system, which are the partisan election of judges and the time-limited office term.

Judges or Politicians?

Whether to appoint or elect judges is an age-old debate involving value choices of political independence or public accountability. The Founding Fathers chose a system whereby all federal judges, around 1,200 today, would get their robes through a system of presidential nomination and Senate approval. Texas judges, around 4,000 which is the most of any state in 2017, hold office through the electoral process. It is true that many judges in the Lone Star State receive a gubernatorial appointment to fill a vacant position, but these appointees must face the voters at a partisan election to stay on the bench.

What is wrong with electing judges? According to Craig McDonald, the director of the government watchdog group Texas for Public Justice, "Judges in Texas swing the gavel with one hand and take the money with the other." McDonald's money-grabbing judges have to sweep up the campaign cash if they are to build up an election war chest. As Republican and Democratic judicial candidates, incumbents and challengers must raise campaign money from the usual suspects: fat cats, law firms, corporations, insurance companies, and medical interests. Along with the dollar chase, judges and would be magistrates have to make the political rounds of party gatherings, civic clubs, labor halls, festival events, barbecue joints, and Baptist churches. To many good government types, pleading for campaign cash and pledging party loyalty put sitting judges in a compromised position.

After the 2016 general election, former Republican state Representative Chas Untermeyer (1977-1981) wrote an opinion editorial that appeared in the *Houston Chronicle* in which he called for the end of partisan judicial elections as one way of putting the court emphasis on justice and not politics. Being only one of four states still electing judges as Republicans or Democrats puts Texas as an outlier in America where most legal experts recommend such systems as nonpartisan elections, gubernatorial appointments with legislative approval, and the Missouri merit plan. Under the Missouri plan, a nonpartisan commission and the governor fill a judicial vacancy, but the appointed judge needs to receive a "thumbs up or thumbs down" from the voters at a future retention election.

Along with the dirty business of having to raise campaign funds and to pledge party support to the reds or the blues, sitting judges are at the mercy of wave elections where down ballot judicial candidates are washed into office in a banner year for Republicans or Democrats. In Harris County, the Republican wave in 1994 stripped the robes off many well-regarded Democratic magistrates and the reverse happened to Republican judges in 2016 when Harris County went true blue. One of the recent GOP victims of straight Democratic Party voting in the Houston area was a respected District Judge Ryan Patrick, the son of Lieutenant Governor Dan Patrick. The wave effect on judges may end in the future as Governor Greg Abbott signed a 2017 law that will eliminate straight ticket voting in Texas elections beginning in 2020.

To win most judgeships in the 1900s, candidates had to prevail in the Democratic primary, and today the reverse is true as winning a GOP election is an essential requirement to capturing a state court position. With low turnouts in party primaries and no D's and R's to cue voters, some disasters have occurred as clueless citizens often have gravitated to familiar names in making blind choices. In *The Texas Supreme Court*, James Halley underscores the point that certain recognizable names will attract votes in down ballot office elections. It is memorable that Democrat Warren G. Harding succeeded Texas State Treasurer Jesse James (1941-1977) in office. Robert W. Calvert, who would go on to become a highly regarded jurist and future chief justice, defeated an incumbent Supreme

Court judge in 1950 as he benefitted by having State Comptroller Robert S. Calvert on the same ballot. Haley also indicates that W. Calvert was helped in his judicial race as major advertising spots for Calvert Whiskey played in Texas around election time.

While a few laughs can be had over electing the not real Jesse James or Warren G. Harding or the Calvert confusion over the man or the bottle, a bad joke was played on Texas in 1976 with the election of Don B. Yarbrough to the Texas Supreme Court. Drawing on the similarity between his last name and three-time liberal Democratic primary gubernatorial candidate Donald H. Yarborough and former U.S. Senator Ralph Yarborough, Don B. was a thirty-four-year-old, unknown, unqualified, and unethical candidate hoping for a high court score.

With a name like Yarbrough, he could not lose and did not as the voters selected the Democratic nominee in a judicial contest with no Republican candidate on the ballot. His tenure on the Supreme Court was short lived, however, as Justice Yarbrough resigned six months after taking office to avoid legislative removal on a variety of charges. His successful flight from Texas to Grenada to avoid criminal charges would end when federal marshals arrested Yarbrough in 1983. After being taken back to Texas, the one-time judge faced both state and federal charges resulting in over ten years of prison time for the infamous Yarbrough man.

Set Terms and Low Pay

Should judges have a set number of years in office or be afforded life tenure? Under the U.S. Constitution, federal judges got life, while state judges were given four-to-six year terms under the Texas Constitution with an opportunity to win additional court time. With only federal courts offering judges life tenure and a few states like Massachusetts and New Hampshire providing magistrates with extended tenure to age seventy, the Texas term of six years on high courts is on the short end of all states with New York at 14, Virginia at 10, and Kentucky at 8.

Despite Texas being in step with its peers with a set judicial term and no life tenure does not answer a question first raised by Alexander Hamilton and seconded by Texas Supreme Court Justice W. St. John Garwood (1948-1958). The Hamilton and Garwood questions dealt with the need for citizens to have confidence that the judiciary was offering "blind" or neutral justice for all. Hamilton's backing for life tenure for judges was based on his desire to shield them from either powerful interests or mass passions. Elected twice to the Supreme Court, Garwood came to be an opponent of choosing judges in partisan races and favored a merit system for judicial selection and tenure.

Without life tenure, one can only imagine what would have happened to U.S. Supreme Court Justice Anthony Kennedy, whose swing vote often made a 5-4 conservative or liberal majority ruling. Had the decisional losers either left-wing or right-wing groups had the electoral means to strike down Kennedy at a future election, the Reagan appointee would have never lasted on the court into the time of the Trump presidency. According to Clifton McCleskey, it was Justice Garwood who said, "The greatest deterrent to getting the best judges (on state courts) is the lack of job security." Without greater job security, many qualified potential judges are unwilling to go through the partisan election process. Even those who have, such as former Chief Justices John Hill (1985-1988), Tom Phillips (1988-2004), and Wallace Jefferson (2004-2013), have criticized the Texas system for deterring many of the state's best legal minds who have reservations about kissing babies and lobbyists' backsides.

Along with a fixed number of years in office, low pay for judges has been a second problem plaguing the third branch of Texas government. Supreme Court members have a salary around $175,000, which is above the 50-state average with California paying the most at $220,000 and Mississippi the least at $120,000. Federal judges on the U.S. Supreme Court receive salaries in the

$250,000 range. Former Chief Justice Wallace Jefferson, who had been touted by San Antonio political commentator Rick Casey as a potential 2016 Obama high court nominee, left the Texas Supreme Court in 2013 for personal and family reasons. The much-admired CJ was not specific about why he was leaving the high court, but uncertain tenure and low pay likely contributed to his decision. Not a big believer in electing partisan judges, Jefferson accepted a partnership in a major law firm with a salary expected to be in the millions.

In Texas the bad marriage of set terms and low pay combine to bring about great court turnover, where judges become government in-and-outers leaving for the more lucrative private legal sector. Instead of a high Texas court position being a lifetime career achievement, it becomes a jumping off point for pursuing financial gain or political power. Texas is not the only state to be criticized where university football coaches make millions, but top magistrates are paid under $200,000. The result of this circumstance is the shortchanging of justice for the people, as justice decided by politician judges with ad hoc tenure is justice denied. While some judges leave the high court for the greener pastures of major Houston and Dallas law firms, Judge John Cornyn (1991-1997) left the Supreme Court to pursue his own political ambition. After leaving the judiciary, Cornyn was elected Texas Attorney General in 1998, and then he went on to win U.S. Senate elections in 2002, 2008, and 2014.

Is Justice for Sale in Texas?

According to the CBS news program *60 Minutes,* the answer is "Yes." In two separate investigations of the Texas Supreme Court conducted during the 1980s and 1990s, national network news correspondents came to the conclusion that justice was "bought" in the Lone Star State. The only difference between 1987 and 1998 was in who were the buyers and who were the sellers.

During the 1980s the state of Texas had the national reputation as America's lawsuit capital as the nine judges on the state's highest civil court had strong ties to personal injury lawyers. With thousands of dollars contributed to partisan judicial candidates, plaintiff's attorneys hoped to argue cases before judges they helped to elect. The financial stakes were high as trial lawyers sued major corporations, insurance companies, and medical facilities on behalf of clients. Court victories meant millions to the trial winners and losers. With the plaintiff's side winning two-thirds of the cases, many lawyers walked out of court as rich men.

It was the Texas Medical Association which would lead the political fight against the Democratic Supreme Court and its trial lawyer backers in the mid-1990s on behalf of Republicans and big business. By 1998 the counterrevolution was complete as red interests had defeated the blues and taken control of the Supreme Court. It would be a new day on the high court as corporations, insurance companies, hospitals, and doctors had bought a new brand of justice.

Since nine Republican judges have been on the Supreme Court, the record is clear as judicial decision watchers have noted the high percentage of court verdicts favoring the wealthy and business institutions over individuals and public interest groups. The citizen advocacy organization Texas Watch has carried out any number of studies measuring how favorable high court rulings are to corporations and insurance companies as opposed to consumers and customers. For the period 2000-2010, a Texas Watch study has consumers winning only five times against business and government defendants out of hundreds of cases.

Looking at the two *60 Minutes* reports, the Texas villains were not bad Democratic judges or bad Republican judges, but the partisan election system which breeds unethical behavior and game fixing. On the question of a rigged judicial system, opinion polls among judges, lawyers, and citizens show agreement in the belief that like professional wrestling matches the outcomes are often scripted in advance. Authors Cheek and Champaign end their book on Texas judicial politics by pondering the question, "Will the new politics of judicial elections continue on its current trajectory toward nosier, nastier, and costlier campaigns?" Whether the answer is yes or no makes little difference to average citizens, as justice for all is a fleeting hope for the people within the state judicial system.

Justice for the Masses

In the United States, elites have used the law and the courts as a means to achieve their economic and political ends. Robert McCloskey, author of *The American Supreme Court*, points out that the national government was a big winner over the states in federalism cases during the Marshall Court era (1801-1835). It was the U.S. Supreme Court that was a friend of business and not labor in the half century prior to Franklin Roosevelt's presidential years. Following the election of Dwight Eisenhower and his choice of former Republican Governor Earl Warren as chief justice in 1953, the high court was expected to support established institutions and the status quo.

No one could have predicted that Chief Justice Warren, a law-and-order former California attorney general, would have led the high court into siding with the citizenry and their rights over state government authority and vested interests. Warren's revolutionary rulings in the areas of civil rights, voting rights, and procedural rights in criminal proceedings brought about cries of outrage from Southern elites, Republicans, and the white masses.

The Warren Court's landmark decisions killed off Jim Crow schools, established voting rights for all in elections, and guaranteed legal representation for the poor in state criminal cases. While lionized by civil libertarians, the chief justice was hated by many Americans, and Richard Nixon used his Southern strategy and anti-U.S. Supreme Court campaign based on the issues of states' rights, "law and order," and resistance to racial integration to win the 1968 presidential race. It was the Warren Court that brought many benefits and rights to the powerless and the penniless in America and Texas.

With the coming of post-Warren chiefs Warren Burger, William Rehnquist, and John Roberts, the American court would seldom be a champion for the masses. Hope for equality of opportunity and fair treatment for Texas citizens would have to come from other legal places: a federal court judge in East Texas and the Texas Supreme Court. It is often said that U.S. District Court judges are some of the most powerful people in America whose influence goes unnoticed. This statement generally is true but William Wayne Justice, a President Lyndon Johnson district court nominee in 1968, would become alternately famous and infamous in Texas during his time on the federal bench. Once asked about Judge Justice, Governor Bill Clements called him "Goofy" in light of his rulings that would shake up the state power structure and status quo practices for years. What made Justice so disliked by his detractors was a number of rulings that confounded elites and showed their callousness toward those at the bottom of society.

What did Justice do for the Texas masses? His rulings would force the state to undo many wrongs inflicted on people of color, the children of illegal immigrants, and those behind state prison bars. It was Justice who ordered the Texas Education Agency (TEA) to desegregate its schools in *United States v. Texas* in 1970. The Warren Court in 1955 had turned over the job of overseeing the integration of public schools to federal district court judges "with all deliberate speed." It was Justice who felt that 15 years of foot dragging was long enough, and the TEA had to stop talking about integration and start integrating now. In 1978 Judge Justice would rule in favor of immigrant schoolchildren whose parents were not citizens. It was Justice's decision to declare a state law illegal that allowed school districts to charge a $1,000 tuition fee for each undocumented child's education. The U.S. Supreme Court would uphold the Justice ruling in its 1982 *Phyler v. Doe* decision.

In *William Wayne Justice: A Judicial Biography*, Frank Kemerer gives credit to the LBJ nominee for his rulings on behalf of the political powerless in Texas. In no other area did Justice live up to his name than in his 1980 *Ruiz v. Estelle* decision in favor of prisoners who are the ultimate society outcasts. While many politicians, like Governor Bill Clements, have run campaign commercials showing prisoners busting rocks as a symbol of their toughness on crime, a Texas judge found the state in violation of the Eighth Amendment prohibition against "cruel and unusual punishment" for its incarceration practices.

What was wrong with Texas prisons? It was Justice's judgment that state prisoners were subjected to overcrowded conditions, brutality within the walls, and a basic lack of medical treatment. While Texas officials would claim that the Lone Star State had the best prison system in America, the Ruiz case facts would put the state claim to shame. Trial evidence showed that over 2,000 inmates slept on prison floors with no beds, that incarcerated trustees known as building binders beat their fellow prisoners to keep them in line, and the state system had just two doctors for every 17,000 inmates.

While William Wayne Justice would stand up for the masses in *United States v. Texas, Phyler v. Doe,* and *Ruiz v. Estelle,* it was Texas Supreme Court judges in *Edgewood v. Kirby* in 1989 who issued a landmark decision on behalf of have-not kids living on the poor side of town. What the Texas high court ruled was that state's method of funding public schools based on local property taxes was unconstitutional given the great disparities of wealth between rich and poor school districts. Under Article VII of the Texas Constitution, the state is required to support and maintain "an efficient system of public schools" for all students.

What made the Edgewood outcome so remarkable was that the U.S. Supreme Court had rejected an earlier argument in *Rodriguez v. San Antonio* (1981) that Texas was violating the 14th Amendment rights of school kids living in property poor districts by its local funding formula. It was so unusual to see the Texas high court do what its U.S. high court counterpart refused to do, and that was rule in favor of the masses in a policy area with major economic implications.

The Texas Supreme Court decision in Edgewood pointed out that the district property wealth differential per student between the Alamo Heights I.S.D. and Edgewood I.S.D., both in Bexar County, was over $500,000. Per pupil spending in the districts was $7,233 in the Anglo suburban Alamo district compared to $2,987 in the Hispanic city Edgewood district. This tale of two districts, one rich and one poor, had major consequences for students in terms of their educational experiences and future life prospects for children living in greater San Antonio.

The Edgewood Texas Supreme Court decision has had a similar after-life like many landmark U.S. Supreme Court rulings where the main decision often leads to future judicial rulings and policy actions taken by the legislative and executive branches. This pattern can be traced at the national level in historic decisions on abortion in *Roe v. Wade,* affirmative action in *University of California v. Bakke,* and a police suspect's rights in *Miranda v. Arizona.* The 1989 Edgewood ruling has brought about an ongoing saga played out in the Legislature and the judiciary to make things right for kids from low-income backgrounds at an affordable political and economic price for elites. Since Edgewood, there appears to be an endless chess game played out between school districts and state officials over the issues of education funding and school quality. These back and forth Edgewood moves should take nothing away from the Texas Supreme Court 9-0 decision in what is perhaps its most significant legal ruling in history.

Fourth Branch of Government

It was during the nineteenth century that the German sociologist Max Weber formulated his theory of bureaucracy based on such principles as hierarchy, specialization, and rules that would lead an organization to achieve efficiency. The end of Weber's bureaucracy, efficiency, is not something that many people would associate with large organizations. What is even more ironic is today's call by some to make federal and state governments more like a business. It is, after all, that Weber's bureaucracy refers equally to Exxon-Mobil as it does to the Pentagon for large organizations come in private and public varieties.

To critics of government, the desire for Washington or Austin to go private may be a mistaken wish as 80 percent of new businesses fail in the first year and 95 percent go belly-up in the first decade. What many students of public administration understand is that government agencies are not private sector firms focused on profits alone. It will be interesting to watch how President Donald Trump who was clueless about government before his election operates in this terra nova over the coming years.

Just like the judiciary, the U.S. and Texas bureaucracies are made up of different elements. At the federal level, the four-part bureaucracy is made up of: cabinet departments, such as Education and Energy, regulatory commissions, like Communications (FCC) and Trade (FTC), executive agencies, such as the National Aeronautics and Space Administration (NASA) and the National Endowment for the Arts (NEA), and government corporations, like the Federal Deposit and Insurance Corporations (FDIC) and the U.S. Postal Service (USPS). The oldest and largest parts of the federal bureaucracy are the departments, with State, War (Defense), and Treasury dating back to the first Washington administration. The newest bureaucratic segments are the government corporations that first emerged in 1933 with Franklin Roosevelt's Tennessee Valley Authority (TVA).

Similar to the federal fourth branch, the Texas bureaucracy

has four parts: elected agency offices, appointed service agencies, appointed regulatory commissions, and appointed licensing and accreditation boards. Some of the largest state bureaucratic units have elected office heads who run for four-year terms as partisan candidates with total independence from gubernatorial authority. Among these general office heads are the Comptroller of Public Accounts, who collects taxes, manages state money, and has considerable authority over the biennial budget. The Attorney General is the chief law enforcement officer of Texas, while the Land Commissioner manages state-owned property including coastal beaches. It is the job of the Agriculture Commissioner and his office to oversee laws related to farm and ranch production and to provide consumer protection.

Along with these single elected agency heads are the elected multimember board officials on the Railroad Commission and the State Board of Education. Three railroad commissioners and 15 education board members are elected for four-year terms as Republicans or Democrats to oversee the important policy areas of energy and schooling. Despite its name the Railroad Commission has nothing to do with trains today, but this commission regulates the Texas oil and gas industry. The State Board of Education oversees the largest state bureaucracy, the Texas Education Agency (TEA), which has responsibility for public education.

The second part of the Texas bureaucracy consists of the appointed service agencies, which provide defined goods and benefits to the state and its citizens. Among these service agencies are the Departments of Criminal Justice, Health and Human Services, Housing and Community Affairs, Parks and Wildlife, Public Safety, Transportation, and the Employee Retirement System. Regulatory commissions with members appointed by the governor and approved by the Senate make up the third bureaucratic part. Examples of this third type are the Texas Alcohol Beverage Commission, Texas Environmental Quality Commission, Department of Insurance, and Public Utility Commission. The general task of these regulatory bodies is to protect consumer rights and to regulate certain industries. In each case, the approved commissioners have autonomy from the elected branches to carry out the duties of their offices in what should be in the public interest.

The fourth and final element of the Texas bureaucracy is made up of appointed licensing and accreditation boards. These boards provide licensing for various occupations and have the authority to investigate any customer or consumer complaints. Examples include the Boards of Nursing, Education Certification, Appraiser Licensing and Certification, Medical, Optometry, and Dental Examiners. After appointment, board members cannot be fired from their offices. Without removal power or the authority to issue executive orders, governors must hope they have chosen well or they may be facing an army of Herman Melville's fictional character "Bartleby," an office employee bent on obstinacy and independence.

How Many? And How Much?

Plenty of myths abound about the number of federal and state bureaucrats and how much money they make. If it were up to Tea Party groups, bashing bureaucrats would become a future Olympic sport. Rhetoric aside, how many people work for Washington and Austin and how well paid are they? The answer may be surprising unless you subscribe to the theory that the only good bureaucrat is a dead bureaucrat as many free market zealots do. Within the federal government, the total number of civil servants has been a flat line for decades at around 2.7 million. Over the years these federal employees have been used as political punching bags by presidential candidates of different partisan stripes from George Wallace to Jimmy Carter to Ronald Reagan.

In Texas the number of state government workers is in the range of 310,000 which is a modest number given the state's growing population and the increasing needs for public services.

Looking at the average salaries for federal and Texas government employees shows a big contrast. For U.S. civil servants the average yearly pay is some $86,000, and for state workers the average salary is around $39,000. While the health and retirement benefits of Washington employees often outstrip what many people receive in private sector jobs, Texas employee benefits are nowhere near their federal counterparts. As a matter of fact, Austin offers its workers some of the smallest benefit packages among the 50 states.

Despite the reality of modest pay and meager benefits, Texas economic and political elites have not passed up many opportunities to bash bureaucrats and their unions. Elite fanning of the flames of anger among nongovernment employees, who are often working as independent contractors for minimum wages and no benefits, has been a successful tactic by establishment figures who want to pit private employees against public employees in the race to the bottom. Having sat in on meetings with Tea Party leaders in Montgomery County, one of the authors (BL) has heard the anger expressed about the overpaid and underworked teachers at the local community college.

Pay issues aside, the work of the 300,000 plus state employees makes up the administrative arm of Texas government, and this fourth branch has a tremendous impact on residents' lives. While the four state bureaucratic parts are technically in the executive branch, the governor has little authority or power beyond the appointment of personnel. Without the ability to issue executive orders or to fire any Bartlebys, the elected chief executive is in a weak position vis a vis the bureaucracy. Like the governor, the Legislature finds itself with a weak hand in terms of state administrative bodies. In theory the House and the Senate have oversight authority over state agencies, commissions, and boards. Due to the reality of a 140 day session every two years, however, legislators find that investigating bureaucratic actions takes a backseat to more pressing state government spending and taxing decisions.

A generation ago the Harvard political scientist Richard

Neustadt gave a warning about a modern government problem that existed between elected officials: presidents, senators, and representatives and entrenched officials: civilian and military bureaucrats. Neustadt's concern was that elected politicians, the temporary above ground government, would not be able to manage and control bureaucrats, the permanent below ground government. Should elected officials fail to check entrenched officials, the loss to America would be democratic decision-making. This warning has not gone unnoticed by experts of public administration.

In Texas the Neustadt problem is magnified many times over given the weak governor's office and part-time Legislature. While the press and the public pay a great deal of attention to the impact of campaign contributions on the votes of elected officials, there is little attention given to the interactions between lobbyists and agency officials. What special interests want to do is to influence the work of state bureaucrats as they go about their jobs of interpreting laws and applying agency rules and regulations in matters of utmost concern.

The powerful want their lobbyists to develop a cozy relationship with agency officials charged with state policy implementation. In an effort to establish this relationship, lobbyists attend administrative hearings, testify about how to carry out certain laws and rules, and submit written recommendations to state authorities. The hired heads will meet face-to-face with agency officials, who often have been appointed from the same sector that the outside influencers are now representing. This agency-networking situation of present outsiders trying to convince former outsiders-now-insiders about the needs of the insurance, banking, and energy sectors of the state has a surreal quality. This make-believe world of pseudo checks and balances among state administrators and economic group representatives is one of the hidden stories of how Texas government works.

The Predatory State

With little executive or legislative oversight of the bureaucracy, well-heeled client groups and special interest lobbyists have turned Texas into a predatory state through their ability to gain significant power over administration agencies. With few checks and balances in place, lobbyists have provided campaign contributions to elected officials who then have proceeded to appoint agency members who are friendly to elites and their goals of increasing profits and wealth.

The result of this subgovernment arrangement that creates a closed circle around elites, politicians, and bureaucrats is to bring about a predatory state environment. Economist James K. Galbraith of the University of Texas has described a predatory state as a "form of corporate control…where the activities of government…are opportunities for profit." According to Galbraith, a predatory state has an economic system where the private or business sector feasts upon the public or government sector for its own financial gain. This state system is where Texas stands today as wealthy interests make off with financial favors from government.

Two manifestations of the predatory state have been economic deregulation and the government privatization of public services. Since the 1990s the political movement backing deregulation and privatization has been led by Republicans and Wall Street Democrats. The effects of these two policies have been great for the haves but costly for the have-nots. In Texas deregulation and privatization have meant more profits for predators and more grief for everyone else.

In 2003 the deregulation of electricity rates came to the Lone Star State. Electricity deregulation arrived at a time when Texans had some of the lowest utility bills in the nation. The promoters of deregulation, such as Governor George W. Bush, believed that things would get even better for consumers without government regulation. An unregulated or free market promised to bring more company providers, greater competition, and lower prices to Texas.

It is true that deregulation did bring more companies into the state, but consumer rates have increased not decreased, so that deregulated areas pay as much and often more than the national average price for home electricity. Through all of this, electric company profits, especially for CenterPoint and TXU, have increased significantly. It was in 2014 that CenterPoint allegedly overcharged its customers by exceeding lawfully allowed rates with company executives even bragging to investors about the coup. When this coup became general knowledge, the Public Utility Commission (PUC), which still had some regulatory authority, refused to look into the matter. At the time of the PUC's refusal to look into the business practices of giants CenterPoint and TXU, the latter company had 86 lobbyists in Austin being paid around $6 million to protect its private interest.

Once upon a time, Texas insurance companies were not able to raise rates without a hearing before the state Department of Insurance Board. After deregulation these hearings were no longer necessary. In 2014 the big three insurance companies moved to raise their costs to the insured. After receiving a 20 percent increase the year before, State Farm announced a 9.8 percent rate hike. For Farmer's Insurance, the ante would go up by 14.9 percent with Allstate settling on a 6.5 percent rate increase. The state's Public Utility Counsel Office, an agency created to represent consumers, objected to the big three's proposed rate hikes and claimed there was no evidence justifying the increases.

In the past the Insurance Commission would have called a hearing to determine whether the increases were warranted. But this time around, the commission was silent and allowed the higher rates to go into effect. What deregulation meant in this case was gains for major insurers and losses for average consumers. It is worth noting that as many as ten percent of state legislators work in some capacity for the insurance industry.

If deregulation has meant more money for Texas upper dogs, then privatization has been a cash cow milked by economic elites.

Under privatization, nongovernmental institutions receive contracts from Austin to do government work. The theory of privatization posits the belief that business firms can do a better job in providing public services in a more efficient and less costly manner than government agencies. In twenty-first century Texas, Republicans, who are in charge of all three branches of state government, are devout members of the church of privatization. This mixed marriage of private to public has been a bonanza for corporate predators in the state. In 1997 the Texas Health and Human Services Commission contracted with Anderson Consulting to computerize child support payments for $11 million. This $11 million state contract ballooned up to $45 million with the firm falling three years behind schedule before the work was completed.

In 2000 Accenture, the former Arthur Anderson firm of Enron fame, received a $899 million contract to manage the state Child Health Insurance Program (CHIP) and to run call centers for the Food Stamp and Medicaid programs. After receiving numerous complaints about poor service, the state cancelled Accenture's contract, although the company held on to its other government contracts. With a corporate slogan of "high performance delivered," Accenture proved that "high" can be pretty "low" in some instances.

In 2003 the story of Clarendon Insurance, a New York based company, came out in a Texas House hearing. The Health and Human Services Commission hired Clarendon to run the state CHIP in rural Texas areas. With no offices or employees in the state, the New York Company subcontracted with Community Health System, an Austin company run by Mike and Rhonda Masters. Under the contract signed with Clarendon, the two Masters were paid $200,000 per month as an administrative fee to oversee the program which the couple did from their own kitchen.

Upon questioning before the House General Investigating Committee in 2003, Mike Masters told a committee member (Author KB) that his company's main job was to answer the phone when someone called which seldom occurred. Masters compared his company's oversight role to that of a homebuilder for as long as the house looks good than the builder has nothing more to do. In time the government contract with the Masters was terminated, but only after millions had been spent by the state for an expensive phone service.

In 2006 Texas signed a $863 million contract with IBM to consolidate state data centers. Within two years the IBM server crashed leading to a data loss and a compromising of fraud investigations. After IBM reached a settlement with the state, the work was transferred to the Xerox Corporation. Acting on behalf of state government, Xerox approved thousands of unnecessary health care requests and rubberstamped many fraudulent claims. It took until 2014 for Texas to drop Xerox and to hire Accenture which had established itself back in 2000 as one of the state's low flyers.

What is wrong with the Texas administrative state? Media organizations as varied as the liberal *Texas Observer* to the conservative *National Review* to the establishment *Texas Tribune* can all agree that something is not right in the Lone Star State with the way the bureaucracy works. In 2003 the *Texas Observer* wrote about companies like Clarendon cashing in on the state CHIP. In 2015 the *National Review* wrote that "Texas has a corruption problem." In 2015 the *Texas Tribune* described many of the administrative agency problems that allowed companies to get fat from government contracts. The ultimate cause for this private sector waste, fraud, and abuse stems from the weakness of Texas government oversight where the governor has no real executive authority over the bureaucracy, the legislature does not have the time needed to provide strong agency reviews, and the courts can only react and not act in keeping predators at bay. This state government configuration of a cozy relationship between private contractors and public agencies has led to a feeding frenzy for Texas tax dollars. The *Texas Tribune* has said it best in an article with the headline: "In State Contracting, Failure is an Option."

Bureaucracy and the Masses

In America and Texas, the main job of elected and appointed government officials is to fulfill their legal responsibilities in a professional manner. The fact that this occurs regularly may be a shock to the legions of government critics in the country. Why more credit is not given to federal and state bureaucrats for the work they do has less to do with poor performances and more to do with the blind ambition of candidates committed to winning at all costs. Building on the manufactured stereotype of a worthless bureaucracy, politicians will launch vitriolic campaigns against government boogeymen as a way of attracting votes. There will be no pushback from bureaucrats against this distorted view as agency officials are dependent on elected legislators and executives for budget funding each year. Behind closed doors, elected officials will reassure entrenched officials not to take all this campaign slander too personally as "it's just politics!"

In Texas showing support for the bureaucracy is akin to being for war and pestilence. The irony in the Lone Star State is that citizens report positive experiences in their face-to-face dealings with state workers, while holding negative views about the behemoth fourth branch of government. It is true that the masses have been hurt by the Texas predator state and elite government control, but the people do benefit by the work civil servants do to improve the social, economic, legal, and educational areas of their lives.

While professional bureaucrats change lives for the better every day, civil servants also have changed history through their willingness to expose government corruption and illegal actions. It was the act of Defense Department analyst Daniel Ellsberg, the leaker of the *The Pentagon Papers* to the national press, who exposed the lies and lawlessness of the Vietnam War. It was the secret meetings of FBI agent Mark Felt, the "Deep Throat" source for *Washington Post* reporters, that ended the crimes of the Nixon presidency. It was George Green, the most famous Texas whistleblower in history, who sent shock waves throughout Austin and brought an unexpected legislative response.

In 1989 George Green was a state architect working in the Texas Department of Human Services. Green reported to his government agency that illegal acts had taken place on state construction sites. It was Green's contention that private contractors were giving cash and gifts to Texas officials to look the other way and not to report job site violations. Despite his good work record, Green was fired and then sued the state under the 1983 Texas Whistleblowing Act, a law protecting state employees from termination for reporting illegalities. The court fight between the architect and the state ended with a $13.7 million judgment in Green's favor. Barbara Jordan, a towering Texas figure of public integrity, testified on behalf of the fired public employee at his civil trial. This $13.7 million award for doing the right thing will be the largest ever under the Texas Whistleblowing Act as the 1995 Legislature changed the law. In a true sign of "no more whistling," the House and Senate capped the future award at $250,000 for those courageous souls willing to come forward with evidence of government corruption.

Concluding Remarks

To the average citizen, the judiciary and bureaucracy are mazes of confusion. With two court types containing five tiers, the 1876 Constitution established a third governmental branch which has become steeped in politics and power. The political aspect means that judges must become partisan candidates running to win and retain office. Many outside observers, such as *60 Minutes* in 1987 and 1999, have questioned the impartiality of the Texas Supreme Court and its decisions. While elites seldom lose in state courts, the masses have achieved judicial victories in the past from the federal rulings of Judge William Wayne Justice and the state high court decision in *Edgewood v. Kirby*. For Texans, a fog hangs over the state bureaucracy as few know much about the size, cost, or work of the fourth branch. With little gubernatorial or legislative oversight authority over governmental agencies, Texas has become a predatory state where private profiteering flourishes. Despite the negative opinions about bureaucracy, state civil servants do meaningful work for all, and whistleblowers like George Green are the genuine heroes of Texas.

Works Noted

Hamilton, Alexander. 1961. *The Federalist Papers*. New York: Signet Classics.

Cheek, Kyle and Anthony Champagne. 2005. *Judicial Politics in Texas*. New York: Peter Lang.

Haley, James L. 2013. *The Texas Supreme Court*. Austin: University of Texas Press.

McCleskey, Clifton. 1963. *The Government and Politics of Texas*. Boston: Little, Brown and Company.

McCloskey, Robert G. 1960. *The American Supreme Court*. Chicago: University of Chicago Press.

Kemerer, Frank R. 1991. *William Wayne Justice*. Austin, University of Texas Press.

Galbraith, James K. 2008. *The Predator State*. New York, Free Press.

CHAPTER TEN

Texas: State of Mass Delusion

As the novelist Gore Vidal once referred to America as the "United States of Amnesia," we will refer to Texas in this chapter as a "State of Mass Delusion." In America and in Texas, elites have created the conditions of historical amnesia and delusional thinking by their power to shape general attitudes and to control specific ideas resulting in the public's acceptance of the economic and political status quo.

The wealthy's influence over the agents of political socialization from the family to schools to churches to the mass media has contributed to American and Texan narratives that often are at odds with the physical reality for millions of people. The American dream and the Texas miracle are now fictions and mirages for the economic bottom half of the population. It has been said in 2017 that to realize the American dream the average person would have to move to Canada. For average Texans, Rick Perry's miracle has been exposed as a backlot movie set produced by Governor "Oops."

Two Lone Star States

In his book on public opinion, Walter Lippmann wrote about "the world outside and the pictures in our heads." Lipmann suggested that people operate in a world of myths and stereotypes, and human beliefs and actions often generate from this pseudo-reality. It is true that in Texas today there are two parallel states existing side by side: the world of the have-mores and haves and the other world of the have-somes and have-nots.

Back in the 1960s, Americans woke up to Michael Harrington's "Other America," where millions of the invisible poor experienced lives of misery in an affluent U.S. society that found the white upper and middle classes living lives of plenty. Historians credit Harrington with inspiring the Kennedy and Johnson administrations to create domestic programs directed at improving the lives of the poor: whites in Appalachia, blacks in ghettos, and browns in barrios.

The two Lone Star states of the haves and the have-nots have been captured in two books on Texas politics published in 2013 and 2012. If Erica Greider's *Big, Hot, Cheap, and Right* would make even miracle man Perry blush, then Gail Collins' *As Texas Goes* would put a frown on the governor's face. While Greider's book could be a Texas Association of Business bestseller, the Collins' work might be branded as "fake news" by Texas Trumpers. With two so divergent views of the state, the logical questions are: Who's right? Who's wrong? The surprise answer is that both authors are right as they are describing the two different Texas worlds of elites and masses.

For most people outside of Texas, it is the Lone Star State of elites that they have come to understand as the true state of the state. Republicans and business representatives have been world-class promotors of the Texas model as the wave of the future. This model, according to its backers, has transformed Texas into a place where life is good because of free enterprise, little government, low taxation, few regulations, and no unions. In his last years in office, Governor Perry said that the Texas way of small government is the answer to the state's prosperity and freedom, while the California way of big government has killed the American dream for people living in the nation's largest state.

Perry's vision of Texas does exist for the have-mores and haves of the state who were identified in Chapter One as Texans with seven and six-figure annual incomes. These Lone Star residents are overwhelmingly white, Anglo, Republican, conservative, professional types employed in the fields of business, finance, law, and medicine. Many of these people are not native Texans, but their professions brought them to the state. Once here the transplanted professionals fell in love with Texas as its rewarding economic environment seemed like manna from heaven. This manna for the haves comes from a recipe based on private fulfillment. It may initially trouble some upper dogs over the lack of Texas public services, but this concern disappears over time as the well-off realize that their own private resources can fill in the state's many policy cracks.

With the traditional Texas philosophy of hating government, some Anglo professionals may be in disagreement with the haters, but they do tend to come around to the anti-state belief system. What converts some of the professionals is the reaping of private benefits in the form of housing, schools, transportation, health care, recreation, and neighborhood security. Over the years the elite belief in privatization has its rewards for the rich as million-dollar homes in the plush parts of cities and suburbs can be mind changers.

Any attempt by do-gooders and labor Democrats to say that state and local governments should do more for those of modest income goes nowhere. It is the genuine belief of the haves that they alone are responsible for their success. In the words of millionaire Clayton Williams, "If you don't have an oil well, get one." The Williams' advice to the have-nots is unrealistic, but what is real to the Anglo haves is their strong opposition to increased government services for the minority have-nots. These added services would mean an increased tax bill for programs they do not need or want others to have if the tab ends up with them.

The have position against government services for the have-nots is clear. For the haves, what good will these services do for "me" and my family, because I live in my own home in a nice neighborhood; I drive an SUV on the toll road to work; my family physician attends my church; I have club memberships and a backyard pool for recreation; my civic club pays for added police patrolling; and I have a camera security system watching over my house. From a pure self-interest standpoint, these arguments are powerful reasons to go private, especially if you attend a megachurch based on the prosperity gospel. Life is good, indeed, in elite Texas.

The Mass State

While elites reap great benefits in the Lone Star State, it is the masses who endure life as a fifth rate existence by social science measures. By fifth rate, we mean that on comparative state domestic indicators, Texas falls into the bottom ten state category. When it comes to quality of life measures, the Lone Star State has nowhere to go but up. To paraphrase Governor Ann Richards' 1988 remarks about President George H.W. Bush, the Texas haves woke up on third base and thought they had hit a triple, while the state have-nots have trouble getting to first base.

The immobility of the masses comes from their family class backgrounds and the lack of government services directed their way. It is no secret in America that the middle class has been vanishing over the past twenty years. Public and private sector decisions have resulted in the growth of U.S. economic inequality. Throughout time, the explanatory power of social class in America has never received the attention it deserves, because the single best predictor for life success is family background. The chance for future economic success for the offspring of the haves has always been good, but for those born into modest or poor families the odds are against rising very high in life. Elite advantages are hard to dismiss, but some of the masses do beat the odds.

How do the masses succeed in elite Texas? One would like to preach the virtues of hard work as the explanation, but social scientists are more apt to say that hard work leads to muscle soreness and not upward mobility. Without the benefit of birth privilege and our depreciation of hard work, how can the masses achieve a better life in the Lone Star State? The answer will not please libertarians, but government programs and public services in the past have meant a decent chance in life for millions of mass citizens. FDR's New Deal and LBJ's Great Society domestic programs gave hope and opportunity for working people. Today the general economic condition looks bright for elites and dark for the masses. Among the fifty states, Texas ranks near the very top as having the greatest income equality gap between its rich and poor citizens.

What does Texas government do for the have-somes and have-nots to improve their lives? The answer is as little as possible unless federal and state courts order it to do something. Looking at comparative state figures on equality of life measures places Texas into the dystopian Trump world. Only the classic refrain of "Thank God for Mississippi" spares the Lone Star State from being the stingiest state in America in addressing the needs of the poor. According to the 2013 "Texas of the Brink" report of the Legislative Study Group, "In Texas today, the American Dream is distant. Texas has the highest percentage of uninsured adults…is dead last in the percentage of high school graduates…generates more hazardous waste and carbon dioxide emissions than any other state."

Even after the Affordable Care Act became law in 2010, Texas still had the highest percentage of adults and children without health insurance in the nation. Texas chose not to expand Medicaid under the ACA that denied insurance to tens of thousands.

Medicaid in Texas currently covers around four million poor, disabled, and elderly state citizens. Expanded Medicaid for the 31 states choosing to opt into the program meant no state costs until 2020 with Washington paying 90 percent after that date. It is estimated that the 19 states, which failed to approve expanded coverage for low-income people, meant the loss of 90,000 lives. Due to this situation and other reasons, 4.3 million Texans have no insurance resulting in, according to Dr. Hagog Kartanjian of the MD Anderson Cancer Center, a "deplorable" state health-care system.

In addition to the health area, the LSG report pointed out the continuing Texas shortcoming in public education which was no doubt made worse by the 2011 draconian $5.4 billion school budget cut. Despite the closed minds of most Austin Republicans, money does make a difference in education. The standard approach of underfunding schools will only perpetuate the Texas situation of a public education system ranked in the bottom 10 of the states, a low high school graduation rate, low college SAT scores, and a high percentage of incoming college students needing educational remediation.

If these conditions were not bad enough, a real shocker about public education was uncovered in 2017 by *Houston Chronicle* reporter Brian Rosenthal. His investigative reports showed that for 12 years the Texas Education Agency had capped special education enrollments in K-12 classes arbitrarily at 8.5 percent, far below the 13 percent national average. This previously hidden cap denied educational opportunity to the least among us—students with disabilities in an action the *Chronicle* called "Humanity Denied." As writer Molly Ivans once said of Republican Governor Bill Clements and the Democratic Legislature, "To get this Governor and Legislature to raise taxes (to help poor and needy folks), you have to hold a gun and a court order to their heads and be ready to use both."

If the poor public health and educational systems have not kept the masses down, then the state environmental conditions of bad air and bad water will cut out the legs from under the have-somes and have-nots. It is the people of Texas who are paying the price for the wealth acquired by oil and chemical companies. Residing in Texas is a health hazard for the masses working and living in urban areas. Due to the toxic environment, the cancer risks are high for urbanites because of the high air pollution levels and the great number of carcinogens in the water and in the land. It may be of little consolation to Texans to know that Chinese citizens live under worst conditions. Because of their affluence and life styles, wealthy individuals are able to reduce their health risks, which is something average residents are unable to do given their incomes, jobs, and neighborhoods.

Exit, Voice, and Loyalty

Having described the two Lone Star States, a question now can be raised about the public acceptance of the status quo which is so beneficial to the haves and so costly to the have-nots. Are the people aware of the state of things or do they operate under a set of myths and illusions that wall them off from the political and economic realities in Texas? This question is impossible to answer with any certainty, but we will apply Albert Hirschman's ideas of exit, voice, and loyalty to provide some insights into mass behavior.

In looking at organizations and systems, Hirschman suggests that individuals have two choices to make in reaction to a deteriorating state of affairs; they can exit and leave the situation or they can use voice and stay to work on changing things. Exit and voice operate within a situational field of loyalty or passivity, where many wait patiently in the hope that things will just get better. For the masses who have come to the conclusion that Texas is a hopeless state, leaving or physically exiting for greener pastures elsewhere does happen. Each year over 400,000 residents say "Adios" to the Lone Star State for any number of reasons.

A move from Texas is impossible for many, however, because home is still home and leaving is not a real option. What is possible and often happens is people take a psychological exit and check out from any connection with public affairs. It may be out of ignorance, apathy, or alienation, but millions disengage themselves from the political system. In spite of the bleak Texas economic environment where one in 12 workers makes the minimum wage of $7.25 per hour, these 450,000 Texans and other low pay employees are mostly indifferent to politics: no registration, no voting, no protests, and no unions. Given the personal costs and risks of political involvement, many wrongly assume that it is just not worth the effort as things will never change in Texas. If not politics then what occupies the lives of the politically indifferent outside of work? Indifferents focus on personal pursuits such as family and friends, church and neighborhood, sports and hobbies, music and media, and beer and barbecue.

While the exiters can choose physical or psychological flight from the public landscape, Hirschman's voice is the political option for people acting to change or reform an unacceptable status quo. Historian Max Krochmal has written about the 1930s to 1960s story of community organizing and civil rights activism to improve mass lives in *Blue Texas*. Through voting and peaceful demonstrations, black, brown, and white activists joined together in multi-racial coalitions to defeat Jim and Juan Crow, to improve mass economic lives, and to challenge an unjust legal system.

Voice is an answer for the have-somes and have-nots unhappy with elite Texas. Given today's red domination of Texas government, political reform movements need to be issue orientated as opposed to partisan-based. Republican Party leaders will discount any reform movement that they associate with the Democratic Party. A quick political math lesson that one of the authors (BL) uses in his classes is to ask students to add two plus two and give the answer. Students laugh and shout out "four," but in the age of Trump this is not the correct answer. For Republicans two plus two equals three and for the Democrats two plus two equals five. The reds and the blues have their own mathematical systems with pat answers which bear no relationship to standard arithmetic. For groups desiring to reform things in Texas, it probably is best to embrace the Republican system of fake math as the best starting point for change.

It is reasonable to say that most Texans display neither exit nor voice as they relate to the state political situation, but an unconscious or conscious loyalty to an elite-dominated government system. As we know in Houston, no matter if it is Trump or Clinton, Abbott or Davis, or Turner or King, we are still confronted with heat, traffic, and cockroaches. This quality of acceptance appears to be a contagion in Texas. On political scientist Lester Milbraith's ladder of political activity from the lowest rung of voting to the highest step of running for office, Texans show a definite fear of heights and seldom get off the ground. In many areas of life, loyalty is to be admired, but mass political allegiance to past Democratic elites and to present Republican elites has been misguided. This mass misguidance may stem from the power of the few to create a state of delusion for the many.

Mass Transformation of Texas

Just How Stupid Are We? is the question raised by historian Rick Shenckman in his book on public opinion, and his answer is "pretty stupid." In facing the truth about the American voter, Shenckman paints a bleak picture of millions of citizens simply not knowing the most elementary facts about government institutions and societal issues. Conservative satirist H.L. Mencken once wrote that no one ever lost money by underestimating the intelligence of the American people.

If older Americans are lost when it comes to political matters, then perhaps the nation will be saved by the millennials and their use of digital technology to create an informed public. According to Mark Bauerlein, this is the wishful thinking of old professors experiencing a senior moment as he characterizes the under 30 set as *The Dumbest Generation.* In his book on young Americans and the digital age, Bauerlein believes that the young are "hooked" on social media which has the effect of stunting their intellectual growth and adult development.

While the views of Rick Shenckman and Mark Bauerlein offer a dark portrait of citizens and civic knowledge, this condition is not a death sentence for democracy in Texas. Both small and large steps can be taken by the Lone Star masses and their potential allies to improve the state political environment. The old Chinese saying of a journey of a thousand miles begins with a single step applies to the have-somes and have-nots in terms of their relationship with the governmental system. In Chapter Three on voting, it was noted that Texas has an abysmal state voting record. To bring about a mass transformation of Texas, the starting point has to be the turning of millions of unregistered citizens into registered voters. A massive increase in registered Texans and voting Texans could deliver a punch to the midsection of the establishment.

Without a push, many Texans will continue to be nonvoters and elites will look right past them as if they did not exist. The push to vote in elections needs to come from the nonpartisan circles of schools, churches, government, and the press. The act of registration and voting should be presented as an act of patriotism and not partisanship. As an army officer in Germany, one author (BL) was his unit's voting officer who used platoon leaders and squad leaders as voting registrars to insure that all soldiers became registered voters. Teachers, ministers, civil servants, and reporters can do likewise in an effort to get more registered and voting Texans.

While millions of citizens fail to vote and do not think much about it, this act of refraining from casting a ballot has negative consequences for their lives. It may be that many people want nothing tangible from government in the form of programs and services, but they still are subject to state actions often to their detriment. Governments are capable of doing things "for" and "to" citizens. The "for" refers to public services provided to citizens to make for better lives. The "to" refers to government restrictions and compliances related to citizen behavior.

The payment of state taxes is the biggest government imposition on the daily lives of Texans. It is within the state tax system that economic and political elites have laid the greatest burden on hourly, low income workers. In Chapter Six it was noted that Susan Pace Hamill listed Texas among the "sinful six" tax states. Since the Hamill book was published, the tax system on low income people has gone from bad to worse. In a state where close to 10 percent of residents are without a checking or savings account, Texas continues to rely on a regressive sales tax for close to 60 percent of its government revenue.

In his book *State Tax Policy*, David Brunori identifies the state sales tax as the most unfair way of raising government revenue. Why do state legislators resort to this unfair tax as opposed to some other just alternative? One of Brunori's explanations for this choice is that it is good politics for politicians concerned only about reelection. Should they move to tax fairness, politicians know the opposition they will face from monied interests which in the past have mounted rich people's movements, according to Isaac William Martin, to untax the top one percent.

It is easy to continue to embrace a regressive tax structure in Austin as the rich and well-connected are not about to become champions of progressive tax reform which would guarantee them higher state taxes. In the absence of tax fairness, local governments are caught into raising property taxes and local sales taxes which hurt the economic lives of the masses. As it is, Texas comes in at the high end of the states with its 6.25 percent sales tax rate. When cities add a local sales tax to the state tax, the percentage is over 8 percent with the tax in Houston, Dallas, and San Antonio at 8.25. This 8.25 percent tax is not a small amount for low income people to pay on their consumer purchases.

The high Texas sales tax and high property taxes in urban counties paid by homeowners and renters alike takes a good slice out of a working family budget. Along with high sales and property taxes, state and local governments have gone to enacting high user fees for past low or no fee citizen services. It can be said on behalf of the average Texan that seldom have so many paid so much in taxes and fees for so little in return.

With today's college degree being the equivalent of the high school degree of a generation ago, the state's retreat from supporting students in higher education is chilling. In 2003, the Texas Legislature moved to deregulate public college and university tuition rates. This decision for the millennials was an economic stab in the back as tuition rates have skyrocketed over 100 percent in 12 years from $1,934 to $4,229 in 2015 at state colleges for a 15-hour course load. The major cause of these increased costs goes back to legislative funding cuts in higher education over the years. The results of these cuts will weigh on Texas students for years to come as the average college loan debt is near $30,000 with close to 60 percent of students having to pay off loans.

Given the Texas historic pattern of doing bad tax things to good working people, this situation can only be changed over time if the nonvoters will go to the polls and throw the "rich" bums out of office. It took little time for national Republicans in 2017 to drop long held party economic and foreign policy positions to fall in line with President Trump's protectionist and isolationist beliefs. If nothing is sacred to national Republicans, then state reds will likely cave in the face of strong political or voting pressures. It may take a decade, but mass voters can transform the Lone Star State from a high tax, low service state into a moderate tax, moderate service state which would be a big improvement for average citizens.

For the masses, voting is an important first step into transforming Texas into a better place for them to live and to raise a family. The mass transformation of Texas cannot take place without a few citizens willing to take a second step forward by running for local government boards and special district positions. There is a need for public-spirited residents to move into the electoral arena and to compete against the usual array of special interest candidates and potential political climbers for grass-roots offices.

Can nonpoliticians committed to the community good make a difference for working people by their presence on local boards? We think so. Back in the early 1980s, political control over the Harris County Municipal Utility District No. 33 (HCMUD 33) rested in the hands of Lincoln Properties, the land development company. As more homes became resident owned, the power shift on the board went from the developer to directors elected by residents. With residents controlling the HCMUD 33 board, the president Janet Stewart decided to think outside of the policy box. What could a water board do to improve people's lives in four starter home neighborhoods resting on a lunar or treeless landscape? Having been abandoned by a homebuilder company which reneged on its promises of playground space and a pool, Stewart and her resident directors met with civic club leaders and homeowners to come up with an answer to enhance community lives.

In two of the subdivisions, there was no place for adults to gather and no place for kids to play. With this in mind, president Stewart instructed board attorney Oliver Pennington, who would later be elected to the Houston City Council in 2009, to see what powers that a MUD had beyond water and sewer services. It was Pennington's view that municipal utility districts had the legal authority to be involved in park services. Based on the attorney's opinion, the MUD 33 board would build and maintain a pocket park on land set aside as open space by the original developer. This first park was built on an area adjacent to the McKamy Meadows and Lincoln Green Estates subdivisions which were neighborhoods without any common space. The official opening of this park named for Nicholas Roman took place in 1987. When Margaret Cox took over as head of the district board, she would oversee the building of the Clarence Evans and Ronald Mumphrey Parks in the 1990s for residents' use.

What leaders Stewart and Cox achieved for the MUD 33 residents was an exceptional example of how citizens inspired by a sense of the public good can accomplish much for working people. The two unsung heroes made their neighborhoods better places to live by showing what local people and a local district government can do. Their public-spiritedness was tested as some citizens argued that the lowering of the tax rate would make more sense as many people would be moving to larger homes in the future and could not take the parks with them. The two presidents held firm against such criticism believing that the handful of dollars returned to individual taxpayers would not be as valuable to the community as parks that people could enjoy forever.

For the mass transformation of Texas into a more equitable state, it will require millions of people to become registered and voting citizens in the future. The second requirement as we have just discussed is for public-spirited people to become members of local boards who have no hidden personal or political agendas in mind. Doing good for the whole community is a good and not a bad thing even if the "Gordon Gekkos" of Wall Street would disagree. The final requirement of mass transformation is for citizens to engage in collective political action to demand that elites do better for all the people living in the Lone Star State.

Life in the state can and has improved for many ordinary Texans through group and collective action at the local level. Neighborhood groups in San Antonio and Houston have shown the way in the past by following the ideas of the legendary Southwest community organizer Ernesto Cortes. Cortes and others laid down the foundations for Communities Organized for Public Service (COPS) in 1974 and The Metropolitan Organization (TMO) in 1979. Both mass groups pressured establishment elites into supporting policy actions to improve people's lives in the Alamo and Bayou cities.

Taking his inspiration from Saul Alinsky, the father of

community organizing, Cortes and religious leaders in San Antonio built a neighborhood organization known as COPS. This organization was based upon a social foundation of Catholic Church parishes and was dedicated to working on daily life issues of traffic, streets, flooding, security, and economic development. It was of particular importance for COPS to stay focused on local issues that could be addressed by city government officials. In their early developmental years, both COPS and TMO stayed away from global issues like world hunger and human rights violations.

What the San Antonio and Houston groups took on were battles with business and government elites over their direct and indirect neglect of the have-nots. Like many places, the two large Texas cities had a political system resembling chamber of commerce democracy. Business elites in San Antonio with their Good Government League and in Houston through the Chamber of Commerce exercised tight control over who was elected to mayoral and council positions and what elected officials could do.

After The Metropolitan Organization was born in 1979, Louis Welch, former Houston mayor and president of the business chamber, was not impressed with the organization and its membership. His reaction to TMO and its government demands, as reported by Mary Beth Rogers in *Cold Anger: A Study of Faith and Politics*, was to say that "the only thing churches are capable of running are school buses and they don't do that very well." Despite the elite naysayers, the goals of COPS and TMO were to improve the standard of living for working class people. The first step in accomplishing these goals was to find natural leaders in the communities of member churches. Cortes and other organizers would motivate these leaders to work on goals important to people such as flooding, local utility rates, garbage collection, traffic, public transportation, and police protection.

The foundation of these local groups was the church base or a pre-existing social network recognizable to all. Ecumenical in spirit, the religious founders of The Metropolitan Organization were Roman Catholic Bishop John Morkovsky, Presbyterian Reverend Dick Siciliano, Methodist lay leader Judge Woodrow Seals, Baptist Minister Bill Lawson, and members of the American Jewish Committee. Faith and politics would be a winning combination especially where political parties played no formal role in nonpartisan elections. Although the Cortes groups did not endorse specific candidates for office, it was clear to their members who were their friends and foes at city hall. What COPS and TMO underscored was the real alignment of Texas politics as presented in this book, which is the vertical perspective of elites and masses and not the horizontal view of left and right. With Catholic and Protestant leaders supporting COPS and TMO, it did put some biblical "fire" under elites to do something for the masses. Should elites be unmoved over mass political requests, ministers always had the statement of Jesus on their side about it being easier for a camel to pass through the eye of a needle than it is for a rich man to get to heaven.

While it surprised some outside observers, local elites did go to work on a number of issues identified by the two mass organizations. In San Antonio COPS brought pressure on city officials and political candidates demanding a simple "Yes" or "No" answer. These questions might relate to their future support or not for specific inclusion of capital improvement projects in a future bond election. Through this exercise, COPS was able to secure millions and millions of bond dollars from San Antonio government officials to be spent on infrastructure projects for low-income neighborhoods.

Although not as successful as COPS, The Metropolitan Organization in Houston has made life better for inner city residents. At its first action convention on October 16, 1982, TMO representatives questioned Kathy Whitmire, the mayor of Houston, and Bill Hobby, the lieutenant governor of Texas, about a number of issues concerning after school programs for latchkey kids, utility costs, neighborhood security, and public transportation. The effect of groups like COPS and TMO has not been to become the new powerbrokers in town, but to get traditional elites to factor in mass interests and concerns into the policymaking equation as a way of improving people's lives.

In Texas over the last generation, COPS and TMO have not been the only nonpartisan groups working to improve mass lives. For over 40 years, the Association of Community Organizations for Reform Now (ACORN) had neighborhood branches throughout the Lone Star State. ACORN's advocacy was directed toward affordable housing, fighting banks over the redlining of certain sections of town, and assisting homeowners to know their rights. Always a strong opponent of the regressive Texas tax structure, the Houston chapter of ACORN was the only organized group to oppose the 1978 Metropolitan Transit Authority (MTA) Plan. Its official "No" position on the transit election plan stemmed from the one cent sales tax increase method of funding the MTA.

In place of the sales tax, ACORN had recommended a combination of new hotel and entertainment taxes to pay for Houston's share of the public transit bill. For Mayor Jim McConn and the Houston Chamber of Commerce, this tax idea was a nonstarter as political and business elites were not about to pay for something that they had hoped to pass off to unsuspecting citizens. While never a favorite organization of the Who's Who crowd, ACORN began to run into trouble with conservatives and Republicans as it branched out into the area of voter registration.

In taking a big step in registering voters, the working-class advocacy group was seen as a radical threat to establishment interests. The end of ACORN came about in 2009 when two right wing zealots posing as a pimp and a prostitute doctored an undercover video that falsely implied the group's compliance in an illegal scheme. After the video appeared on conservative web sites, the false report was picked up by the national news media and broadcast widely. Once this happened, ACORN's financial supporters pulled the plug on its funding. It would take some time for the truth to come out which vindicated the organization of wrongdoing, but by then the group officially had been dissolved.

From the ashes of the Association of Community Organizations for Reform Now would come TOP—the Texas Organizing Project led initially by Ginny Goldman, an advocate of direct action organizing. When asked about the charge that TOP was a Democratic Party front group, Goldman's immediate response was to say that her group's goal was not to turn Texas blue, but to push for policies related to schooling, housing, and health care to help low income people. For positive future changes helping nonelites in Texas, organizations like COPS, TMO, ACORN, and TOP must be active politically in working with and against establishment powers. If community groups are seen as Democratic or Republican Party offshoots, their effectiveness will be compromised in the eyes of many who distrust blue and red partisans to ever do the right thing for the people.

For the Lone Star State to become a true Texas miracle in the future, not just for elites but also for the masses, will require some effort on the part of the general public. The three necessary ingredients we have stated for the mass transformation of Texas are for a substantial increase in voting from citizens of moderate to low income means, for public-spirited neighborhood leaders to win offices on local government boards, and for citizens to embrace collective political action focused on their needs. Should these three ingredients come together, Texas will be transformed into place worthy of praise for its kind heart extended to all of its people both big and small.

Concluding Remarks

Within Texas, the two Lone Star States of elites and masses exist side by side. Life is good in elite Texas where residents do realize the American Dream, but a different life faces those living in mass Texas where the dream has turned into an American Nightmare. While mass acceptance of the economic and political status quo is common, there have been some public displays of exit and voice as two citizen responses to the way things are. To transform Texas into a true miracle state in the future will require a substantial commitment on the part of the have-somes and have-nots to engage in a variety of political activities from voting to collective action. It's time for a Texas Mass-a-Cure! *Now!*

Works Noted

Lippmann, Walter. 1946. *Public Opinion.* New York: Penguin Books.

Harrington, Michael. 1962. *The Other America.* New York: McMillion.

Greider, Erica. 2013. *Big, Hot, Cheap, and Right.* New York: Public Affairs.

Collins, Gail. 2012. *As Texas Goes.* New York: Liveright.

Ivins, Molly. 2013. *Letters to the Nation.* New York: The Nation.

Hirschman, Albert O. 1970. *Exit, Voice, and Loyalty.* Cambridge: Harvard University Press.

Krochmal, Max. 2016. *Blue Texas.* Chapel Hill: University of North Carolina Press.

Milbraith, Lester W. 1956. *Political Participation.* New York: Rand McNally.

Shenkman, Rick. 2008. *Just How Stupid Are We?.* New York: Basic Books.

Bauerlein, Mark. 2009. *The Dumbest Generation.* New York: Tarcher/Penguin.

Brunori, David. 2016. *State Tax Policy.* Lanham, Maryland: Roman & Littlefield.

Martin, Isaac William. 2013. *Rich People's Movements.* New York: Oxford University Press.

Rogers, Mary Beth. 1990. *Cold Anger.* Denton, TX: University of North Texas Press.

BIBLIOGRAPHY

Abbott, Greg. *Broken But Unbowed*. 2016. New York: Threshold Editions.

American Political Science Association Task Force Report. 2004. *"American Democracy in an Age of Rising Inequality."*

Anderson, James E. 1992. *Texas Politics*. New York: Harper Collins Publishers.

Bachrach, Peter and Morton S. Baratz. 1962. "Two Faces of Power." *American Political Review*: 947-952.

Bailey, Stephen Kemp. 1950. *Congress Makes a Law*. New York: Vintage Books.

Barber, James David. 1965. *The Lawmakers*. New Haven, CT: Yale University Press.

Barber, James David. 1972. *The Presidential Character*. Englewood Cliffs, N.J.: Prentice Hall.

Bauerlein, Mark. 2009. *The Dumbest Generation*. New York: Tarcher/Penguin.

Beard, Charles A. 1913. *An Economic Interpretation of the Constitution of the United States*. New York: MacMillan.

Brennan, Jason. 2016. *Against Democracy*. Princeton, NJ: Princeton University Press.

Brunori, David. 2016. *State Tax Policy*. Lanham, Maryland: Roman & Littlefield.

Bryce, Robert. 2004. *Cronies.* New York: Public Affairs.

Cheek, Kyle and Anthony Champagne. 2005. *Judicial Politics in Texas.* New York: Peter Lang.

Clinton, Hillary. 1996. *It Takes a Village.* New York: Simon & Schuster.

Collins, Gail. 2012. *As Texas Goes.* New York: Liveright.

Cox, Patrick and Michael Phillips. 2010. *The House Will Come to Order.* Austin: University of Texas Press.

Crozier, Michael and Samuel P. Huntington. 1975. *The Crisis of Democracy.* New York: New University Press.

Dahl, Robert A. 1967. *Pluralist Democracy in the United States.* Chicago: Randy McNally.

Daley, David. 2016. *Rat F**cked.* New York: Liveright Publishing Corporation.

Davidson, Chandler. 1990. *Race and Class in Texas Politics.* Princeton, NJ: Princeton University Press.

Davidson, Roger H. 1969. *The Role of the Congressman.* New York: Pegasus.

Diamond, Martin. 1981. *The Founding of the Democratic Republic.* Itaca, IL: F.E. Peacock Publishers.

Domhoff, G. William. 1972. *Fat Cats & Democrats.* Englewood Cliffs, NJ: Prentice-Hall.

Dye, Thomas and Harmon Zeigler. 2009. *The Irony of Democracy.* Boston: Wadsworth Cengage Learning.

Dye, Thomas. 2014. *Who's Running America?.* Boulder, Co.: Paradigm Publishers.

Frank, Thomas. 2004. *What's the Matter with Kansas?.* New York: Metropolitan Books.

Frank, Thomas, 2016. *Listen, Liberal.* New York: Metropolitan Books.

Galbraith, James K. 2008. *The Predator State.* New York, Free Press.

Gantt, Fred. 1964. *The Chief Executive in Texas.* Austin: University of Texas Press.

Goodwin, George. 1970. *The Little Legislatures.* Amherst, MA: The University of Massachusetts Press.

Green, George Norris. 1984. *The Establishment in Texas Politics.* Norman. OK: University of Oklahoma Press.

Green, Mark J., 1972. *Who Runs Congress?.* New York: Bantam Books.

Greider, Erica. 2013. *Big, Hot, Cheap, and Right.* New York: Public Affairs.

Gutierrez, Jose Angel. 2005. *The Making of a Civil Rights Leader.* Houston: Arte Publico Press.

Haag, Stefan D. 2006. *Annotated 1876 Texas Constitution.* New York: Pearson-Longman.

Hacker, Jacob S. and Paul Pierson. 2010. *Winner-Take-All Politics.* New York: Simon & Schuster.

Haley, James L. 2013. *The Texas Supreme Court.* Austin: University of Texas Press.

Hamill, Susan Pace. 2007. *As Certain as Death.* Durham, NC: Carolina Academic Press.

Hamilton, Alexander. 1961. *The Federalist Papers.* New York: Signet Classics.

Harrington, Michael. 1962. *The Other America.* New York: McMillion.

Hirschman, Albert O. 1970. *Exit, Voice, and Loyalty.* Cambridge: Harvard University Press.

Hobby, Bill. 2010. *How Things Really Work.* Austin: Briscoe Center.

Holzer, Harold and Norton Garfinkle. 2015. *A Just and Generous Nation.* New York: Basic Books.

Ivins, Molly. 2013. *Letters to the Nation.* New York: The Nation.

Jillson, Cal. 2011. *Texas Politics* New York: Routledge.

Jillson, Cal. 2015. *Lone Star Tarnished.* New York: Routledge.

Kellerman, Barbara. 1984. *The Political Presidency.* New York: Oxford University Press.

Kemerer, Frank R. 1991. *William Wayne Justice.* Austin, University of Texas Press.

Key, Jr. V.O. 1949. *Southern Politics.* New York: Vintage.

Key V.O. Jr. 1958. *Politics, Parties, and Pressure Groups.* New York: Thomas Y. Crowell.

Keyssar, Alexander. 2000. *The Right to Vote*. New York: Basic Books.

Knaggs, John R. 1998. *Two-Party Texas*. Austin, TX: Eakin Press.

Krochmal, Max. 2016. *Blue Texas*. Chapel Hill: University of North Carolina Press.

Lamare, James W. 1981. *Texas Politics: Economics, Power, and Policy*. St. Paul, MN: West Publishing.

Leighley, Jan E. and Jonathon Nager. 2014. *Who Votes Now?*. Princeton, NJ: Princeton University Press.

Lentz, Jacob. 2002. *Electing Jesse Ventura*. Boulder, Co.: Lynne Rienner Publishers.

Lippmann, Walter. 1946. *Public Opinion*. New York: Penguin Books.

Lipset, Seymour Martin. 1963. *Political Man*. New York: Anchor Books.

Martin, Isaac William. 2013. *Rich People's Movements*. New York: Oxford University Press.

McCall, Brian. 2009. *The Power of the Texas Governor*. Austin: University of Texas Press.

McCleskey, Clifton. 1963. *The Government and Politics of Texas*. Boston: Little, Brown and Company.

McCloskey, Robert G. 1960. *The American Supreme Court*. Chicago: University of Chicago Press.

McDonald, Archie P. 2007. *Texas: A Compact History*. Abilene, TX: State House Press.

Milbraith, Lester W. 1956. *Political Participation*. New York: Rand McNally.

Mills, C. Wright. 1959. *The Power Elite*. New York: Oxford University Press.

Monty, Jacob M. 2011. *Hispanic's in the Workplace*. Houston: Emporion Press.

Neustadt, Richard. 1960. *Presidential Power*. New York: John Wiley & Sons.

Novak, Michael. 1978. *The American Vision*. Washington, D.C.: American Enterprise Institute.

Parker, Richard. 2014. *Lonestar Nation*. New York: Pegasus Books.

Perry, Rick. 2010. *FED UP!*. New York: Little, Brown and CO.

Phillips, Kevin. 1969. *The Emerging Republican Majority*. New Rochelle, NY: Arlington House.

Rogers, Mary Beth. 2016. *Turning Texas Blue*. New York: St. Martin's Press.

Rogers, Mary Beth. 1990. *Cold Anger*. Denton, TX: University of North Texas Press.

Rossiter, Clinton. 1960. *The American Presidency*. New York: Harcourt, Brace & World.

Rothkopf, David. 2008. *Superclass*. New York: Farrar. Straus, and Giroux.

Sabato, Larry. 1983. *Goodbye to Good-Time Charlie*. Washington, D.C.: CQ Press.

Sabato, Larry J. 2007. *A More Perfect Constitution*. New York: Walker & Company.

Scammon, Richard M. and Ben J. Wattenberg. 1970. *The Real Majority*. New York: Coward-McCann.

Shenkman, Rick. 2008. *Just How Stupid Are We?*. New York: Basic Books.

Schlesinger, Joseph A. 1966. *Ambition in Politics*. Chicago: Rand McNally.

Squire Peverill and Gary Moncrief. 2015. *State Legislatures Today*. Lanham, MD: Rowman & Littlefield.

Stiglitz, Joseph E. 2016. *Rewriting the Rules of the American Economy*. New York: W.W. Norton.

Texas State Directory 2016, Austin: Texas State Directory Press.

Tolleson-Rinehart, Sue and Jeannie R, Stanley. 1994. *Claytie and the Lady* Austin, TX: University of Texas Press.

Wilson, Woodrow. 1885. *Congressional Government*. New York: Houghton Mifflin Co.

Witcover, Jules. 2003. *Party of the People*. New York: Random House.

ON THE AUTHORS

A lot of lawmakers would give up their cherished parking spaces to have what (Texas Representative) **Kevin Bailey** has going for him: fire in the belly, cleverness, a loyal following, a knack for phrasing a political point, and a booming voice to deliver it.

—*Texas Monthly*, July, 1999

For the past generation, **Bob Locander** has been on the legal and political frontlines for educational employee rights and student interests in the Houston area. He was a plaintiff in a 1980 federal suit against the North Harris County College President and the Board of Trustees over the 1st and 14th Amendment rights of teachers. His campaign work on local elections has contributed to the victories of grassroots challengers over establishment incumbents.

—Attorney Chris Tritico, Labor and Education Law

Richard Shaw has been the public face of the labor movement for decades in Harris County. No one has done more to advance the interests of working people in the Gulf Coast region. In addition to being a leader of the Street Heat and Justice Bus actions, Shaw founded the first Workers Center in Houston that supported the fight to recover stolen wages and to advance workplace rights and job safety.

—President Alan Hall, AFT Local 4518

9 781974 269518